"A passionate call for a faith that goes beyond the nominal, the normal and the nice… If you're tired of the brand of Christianity that hides behind a veneer of respectability and rarely goes more than skin deep, read and heed this invitation to a heartfelt encounter with God, with his people and with your community."

– **Gerard Kelly**, author of *The Prodigal Evangelical*

"Malcolm has managed that most difficult of things – to write a book which is both realistic and readable, and yet which carries great spiritual wisdom."

– **Revd Dr Alison Morgan**, ReSource, author of *The Wild Gospel* and *The Word on the Wind*

Also by Malcolm Duncan:

I WANT TO BE
A GOD GAZER

Yearning for intimacy with the Saviour

Malcolm Duncan

MONARCH
BOOKS

Oxford UK, and Grand Rapids, USA

Published by Monarch Books
an imprint of
Lion Hudson plc
Wilkinson House, Jordan Hill Road,
Oxford OX2 8DR, England
Email: monarch@lionhudson.com
www.lionhudson.com/monarch

ISBN 978 0 85721 481 2
e-ISBN 978 0 85721 482 9

First edition 2015

Acknowledgments
Unless otherwise indicated, Scripture quotations are taken from NRSV Anglicised,
The New Revised Standard Version of the Bible copyright © 1989 by the Division
of Christian Education of the National Council of Churches in the USA. Used by
permission. All Rights Reserved.
Scripture quotations marked NIV taken from the Holy Bible, New International
Version Anglicised. Copyright © 1979, 1984, 2011 Biblica, formerly International
Bible Society. Used by permission of Hodder & Stoughton Ltd, an Hachette UK
company. All rights reserved. "NIV" is a registered trademark of Biblica. UK
trademark number 1448790.
Scripture quotations marked NLT are taken from the Holy Bible, New Living
Translation, copyright © 1996, 2004, 2007 by Tyndale House Foundation. Used by
permission of Tyndale House Publishers, Inc., Carol Stream, Illinois 60188. All rights
reserved.
Scripture quotations marked The Message are taken from The Message. Copyright ©
by Eugene H. Peterson 1993, 1994, 1995, 1996, 2000, 2001, 2002. Used by permission
of NavPress Publishing Group.
Scripture quotations marked ESV are from The Holy Bible, English Standard
Version® (ESV®) copyright © 2001 by Crossway, a publishing ministry of Good News
Publishers. All rights reserved.

p. 136: Extract from *Reflections on the Psalms: The Celebrated Musings on One of the
Most Intriguing Books of the Bible* by C.S. Lewis, copyright © C.S. Lewis Pte Ltd. 1964.
Reprinted by permission of the C. S. Lewis company.

A catalogue record for this book is available from the British Library

Printed and bound in the UK, February 2015, LH26

Contents

Rumours of God and Whispers of Hope

There are many of us who know that the rumours of God's death are greatly exaggerated. God just won't go away. Despite the best efforts of many, the idea of God lives on. Like a word whispered deep in the caverns of the human heart, the idea of God echoes around the chambers of our lives. God's continued vitality is seen in deep and intuitive yearnings placed within the psyches of all people to discover what it means to be authentically alive. Sometimes we call it a search for reality. Sometimes we describe it as finding our true meaning or discovering our genuine purpose. Sometimes we describe it as trying to understand why we are here. The words we use are not the most important thing. It is the sentiment behind them that matters, and that sentiment is the search for significance, for meaning; the quest for the purpose of life itself.

No matter how hard we try, we just don't seem to be able to rid ourselves of the niggling notion that God exists. Like an almost unnoticeable speck of sand placed in the shell of our experiences, the possibility of his existence seems to lie in patient anticipation within each one of us. Most often we know the yearning is present because of a simple grit-like thought in the oysters of our individual consciousness that goes something like this: "There has to be more to life than this."

I knew God was real long before I believed he was personal. As a young boy, growing up in a family that was largely irreligious but had a deep sense of right and wrong, I think the rumour of God was shaping me long before I realized its significance. I caught glimpses of him in my life, but did not understand him. Perhaps it was because I was too young, or too naive. Perhaps it was because his existence seemed so alien to me in the midst of my circumstances. Perhaps it was because I grew up in the culture of Northern Ireland where the religious notions of God had a profound and often negative impact on our culture. I can remember lying in bed at night and wondering what God was like. I don't think I ever thought there was no God, but I was not at all certain what "God" meant. My glimpses of him kept my searching alive, but they did not change my life. I may have glimpsed him many times as I grew up, but I rarely gave him my attention for very long. Perhaps you are like I was?

We occasionally catch a glimpse of what could be a beautiful pearl hidden within the recesses of our thinking. It may be sparked by a moment of family beauty, such as a birth or a wedding. Perhaps it is an important personal landmark in the life of someone we love? We watch a sunrise, or stand alone in the night and look up at the star-speckled sky, and something within us yearns to understand the purpose of it all. Intuitively, we know that the source of our wonder is God, but we have not been sure what God is like because we have not yet come into a personal relationship with him. The beauty we behold and the aliveness of the moment are invitations to wonder at life itself because they come from Life himself. We know it; we just don't always know what to do with such an existential moment.

We know that these encounters are gateways into the shadow of something imprinted within humanity itself. We have guessed that they are the whisper of a voice we have a memory of hearing, but we are not sure where or when. These moments of wonderment are part of a movement that fits into the symphony of life. We realize that God is the Conductor of the music, but we sometimes struggle to hear the notes. We can sometimes feel like we are standing on a stage, trying to remember our lines, and the Prompter is standing offstage with the script in his hands. He is speaking to us, trying to help us without removing our dignity and our humanity and our choice. We know it's God; we just can't always hear him very well. We are familiar enough with his voice to recognize it, but not so familiar with it that we can decipher clearly what he is saying. The impact is that we find ourselves asking the greatest questions imaginable: "How do I encounter God?", "How can I hear him?", and "What can I do to meet him?"

Whispers of hope

The yearning for a deeper encounter with him surfaces at startling moments in our lives. These moments are whispers of hope. They are pivots of destiny upon which the balance of our future lies. These are unmoving signposts that can set the direction of our journey amidst the storms of life – moments such as when we walk away from the funeral of a friend or a loved one. In the unexpected pauses of reflection that accompany such occasions we are confronted with our own mortality, somehow gripped again by this "yearning". Perhaps Jung was right when he argued that the moments at which we are most profoundly confronted with both the inevitability of death and the deep questions of life occur as we watch the last breath leave the body of someone we love or as we see their earthly remains taken from us. Our latent belief in God becomes a desperation for his presence. We know we need him. We pray intuitively. It's funny that for so many people, the first thing they do in a moment of deep sadness and grief is pray. Why is that? The whisper in our souls is finding its own expression in our lives. We know we want God.

Then again, our longing for God lies heavy upon us as we welcome a life into the world. This little person, full of possibility and hope, looks at us with eyes like lasers that pierce the deepest chambers of our soul, searching out our significance, scouring our souls to see where we "fit". Once again Life is encountering us, but we do not know what to do with it.

There are many such pivots and whispers in our lives. Some of them are positive and some of them are negative, but they bring alive in us what we know is there – a hunger for God. They can be the realization that the great change we hoped for didn't deliver on its promises to transform us, or they can be the discovery that the great accomplishment that was supposed to sound the depths of "being alive" actually ended up as nothing more than a tinkling cymbal and didn't reverberate deeply within us at all. We have encountered God enough to accept that he exists, but we have not encountered him enough to change our lives. We have not yet found our fulfilment in him.

Perhaps it was the day we were married, or the day we were divorced? On the other hand, it may have been the day we were awarded our degree or the moment we were appointed to our dream job, or the day we realized we weren't going to pass at all. For some of us, it was the moment we finally paid off the mortgage and we could say the house was really and truly ours – or the moment we lost it all and we wondered how it came to this.

You know better than anyone the moments in your life that have caused you to wonder at life itself. You know your own whispers. You have encountered your own pivotal moments. We all have. We wonder about God. We either don't know how he fits into our lives or we do not want him to fit into our lives because to believe in him would demand a change we are not willing to make, or a step we are not willing to take. He makes us uncomfortable so we would rather get rid of him than embrace him. We know we need him, but we don't want to need him.

God – the body that won't sink

The idea of God, the yearning for him, is like a dead body (or so we assume) that has been heavily weighted with our guilt and wrapped tightly in the brilliant bandages of our intellect then tossed into the deep lake of our memories, where we hope it will sink into the water of our memory and stay submerged forever. The problem is that the body eventually floats to the surface again. The yearning will not go away. Nothing, it appears, will keep it at the bottom of the lake. No weight of our own brilliance is weighty enough. No heavy stone of modern thinking is heavy enough to keep the idea of God out of sight and therefore out of mind. No hermetically sealed box of logic or tightly secured chains of reason will keep him sunken. Nothing, it appears, will keep him down.

The startling thing is this – the corpse is not a corpse at all! If we take the time to fish the body out from the water of our lives, we discover that this cold, lifeless notion is not cold; neither is it lifeless. On the contrary, he is very much alive. He has survived our attempts at drowning and has emerged from the bottom of our thoughts again, his very reappearance being evidence of his continued life. To our dismay, God is cleverer than we are. The bandages of our intellect are no longer shimmering with brilliance. They are tattered, gaping, and worn rags, eaten away by unanswerable questions and the powerful, deep currents of our conscience. What we knew all along is true – God is not dead. This "corpse" is not a corpse at all, and he wants to be untied. He wants us to free him. He has been holding his breath all the time and waiting for us to release him into our lives. If only he would leave us alone, all would be well, but it seems he just won't stay down. He loves us too much to leave us on our own.

Our problem is that what we then tend to do is tie another weight to his body, wrap our reason a little tighter and throw him into the water again. We then watch him submerge again – for a while. We have fallen for the lie that as long as we can't see him, he isn't there. So we sink him again by trying to avoid situations where his body might arise. We rush through the very moments of mystery or questioning in our lives that most fully confront us with our yearnings. Such moments are actually gifts to us that would unwrap a new understanding of God's nearness, but we reject the gifts like unwanted presents. We immerse ourselves in the humdrum rhythm of daily living in the vain hope that the beat of existing will drown out the rhythm of living, but it never does because it never can.

Our yearning for God will not go away.

When I was a little boy and someone I was either afraid of or felt shy around came into the room, I would lift my hands to my face and hide my eyes. My logic was simple: if I could not see them then they would not be able to see me. This common little practice is something that still makes me smile when I see children doing it today. I can remember my own children doing exactly the same thing. It is nonsense, of course, and as we get older we know it is silly and naive, yet many of us do exactly this with God. We cover our eyes before him, hoping that because we cannot see him, he cannot see us. This deeply flawed logic we cling to gives us the freedom of moral blindness and opens the door for us to do whatever we like, whenever we please, in whatever way we want, but it doesn't take the yearning away. The idea that if we cannot see him then he cannot see us just doesn't work because deep down within us we know that there is more. God can see us. God always sees us.

Fulcrums

Our lives are balanced on tiny fulcrums that tilt our destinies one way or another. I am pretty convinced that the most important of these fulcrums are the ones that we tend to brush aside or run away from the quickest. These are the moments when our "yearning" surfaces and we try to sink it again. Instead of allowing it to pierce our hearts, we push it under the water and rush to the next important thing. If we crowd God out, then he will go away. If we make our lives so full that there is no room for anything else, then there will not be any room for him. If our diaries are full, then there won't be any time to think, to reflect, or to wonder. We try to drown God out with busyness. Please don't do that.

This little book is an appeal to you. It's a heartfelt plea, really. Instead of running from the moments in your life when the body surfaces, would you please stop and think about who you are, why you are here, and what your life is all about? Let God show himself to you. Instead of covering your eyes in infantile naivety, would you please look at God and let him look at you?

I would go further. Instead of looking *at* God, look *into* God and let him look *into* you. See what he is really like and feel his deep gaze into your own hidden heart. I think that if you do, you might find that something beautiful begins to happen. Those deep, yearning, aching questions might begin to be answered, and you will never be the same again. Instead of running away from him, just stop. Let him speak to you. Give him the chance to show you what he is really like. Let your yearning shape your living. Let your deep, intuitive conviction that there is a God cut away the weights that have tried to hold God down in your heart. Allow him to rise to the surface again. Let God reveal himself to you. Look at him as he looks at you.

My prayer is that *I Want to be a God Gazer: Yearning for intimacy with the Saviour* will help you to see God again, or see him more clearly. My hope is that you will read the book several times and that you will return to it again and again. You can dip into and out of it at various times. I want to make it as easy for you as possible. I've designed the book around a piece of my writing entitled *God Gazer* so it's worth taking the time to read it several times before you launch into the book itself. Each chapter has a stanza of *God Gazer* at the beginning to help you think and perhaps to pray.

Please try to read this book deliberately and intentionally. Why not try journaling alongside your reading? Or maybe you could try encouraging your friends or members of your small group or church to each buy a copy of *I Want to be a God Gazer: Yearning for intimacy with the Saviour.* You could then read it and discuss it together. Maybe you are a churchgoer but you are yet to have a personal encounter with God. You fear God but you do not know him. If that is true then maybe *I Want to be a God Gazer: Yearning for intimacy with the Saviour* will help you move beyond a formal belief in God into a personal relationship with God. Perhaps the book can help you with your spiritual formation.

However you do it, my hope is that you will allow God to meet you. My prayer is that you will invite him to be the centre of your life. There is a world of difference between a discussion about God and a dialogue with him. Even if you are not used to praying, reading Scripture, or personal reflection, give some time to trying these things. Try reading it in the morning, or in the evening, or on the train, or in the first fifteen minutes of your lunch hour, or when you come back from dropping the children off at school. Just give yourself the luxury of a few moments of quiet and a little bit of space to listen to what God might say to you. Look for what he might show you. God is more eager to meet with you than you are to meet with him. Give him the opportunity to encounter you.

Stop and think. Look for him in the everyday situations and occurrences of your life.

Walk slowly through those moments with your eyes open.

Listen closely to what you might be hearing.

Give God some time.

Where did *God Gazer* come from?

I originally wrote *God Gazer* for a conference I was addressing in January 2010. I was one of the keynote speakers and had been asked to explore the dual themes of the power of God's Word and the importance of an encounter with God. (I capitalize "Word" because I was addressing not only the question of Scripture but also the question of the Living Word, the Lord Jesus Christ.)

I am not sure whether I would describe *God Gazer* as a poem, a prayer, a confession, a liturgy, or a reflection. I don't think it really matters. Somehow, it has touched people around the world. It has been published, shared, spoken, learned, referred to, and quoted on every continent of the globe. For a long time I wasn't really sure why that was happening, but now I think I know why it has touched people. It's the yearning thing. *God Gazer* captures something of the longing of our hearts for God in simple words. It "says" something that is really important. If we want to really live, then we need to be rooted in Life. If we want to know what life is about, then *our* reason must be immersed in the Great Reason, the Logos, and the Water of Life. If we want our lives to be strong and stormproof structures, then we must be built upon the Unshakeable Foundation.

I have changed the order of the stanzas from the original piece to avoid repeating some of my reflections. When you are writing poetry/prose like the original *God Gazer*, repetition is part of the shape and form of what you are trying to say, but when it comes to writing reflections on those stanzas, repetition would become tedious. None of the stanzas have been removed; they have just been moved around a little, and the flow of *God Gazer* as a poem still works very well.

As you read *I Want to be a God Gazer: Yearning for intimacy with the Saviour*, may God draw you more closely into his Story and his Purpose, and may you discover a clearer, more compelling vision for life than you ever thought possible. Why? That's easy to answer: because life can't spring from any other thing. My prayer for you is simple:

May you be captured by the brilliance that springs from the radiance of him.

Malcolm Duncan
Buckinghamshire, Summer 2014

God Gazer

I want to be a God gazer!
Captured by the brilliance
that springs from the radiance
of you.

I want to be a God gazer!
Not a cheap food grazer
or an easy option lazer.
I want to be a trailblazer
for the ordinary, everyday life.

I want to be a God gazer!
Not just copying the halcyon ways
that shimmer brighter in the haze
of bygone rays and the good old days.

I want to be a God gazer!
Looking beyond the trappings of success,
cutting through the stucco of respectability
like a laser piercing darkness.

I want to be a God gazer!
Reaching for the stars and
seeing beauty in the moment by
becoming fluent in the language
of the God who is here, who is now.

I want to be a God gazer!
Until my imagination is saturated;
until my thirst is sated;
until my passion is stirred;
until my intellect is stretched
as far as it can be;
until my yearning yearns
for others to be free.

I want to be a God gazer!
Not a meetings manager
or a people pleaser
or a "tea and sympathy" vicar.
Not a leadership trainer.
Not just a speaker
but a seeker.

I want to be a God gazer…
and for a moment I want God
to gaze through me.
I want others to see
his Eyes,
Heart,
Mind,
and Love
above everything else in me.

I want to be a God gazer!
Captured by the brilliance
that springs from the radiance
of you.

I want to be a Life giver
not a life sucker.
I want my life to be releasing,
not appeasing or placating.

I want to be a Life giver!
A "you can do it" releaser,
a "have a go" preacher,
a "you were born to do this" pastor.

I want to be a Life giver!
Seeing rivers flow, not die,
seeing others rise and fly,
helping friends reach for the stars
even if they sometimes miss,
at least they can say they tried.

I want to be a Life giver!
A drainpipe without blockages,
a circuit without stoppages,
a connector without breakages.

I want to be a Life giver!
Generous in spirit and in heart,
letting the forgotten make a start
at being Life givers, too.

I want to be a Life giver!
Connected to the Source
and pointing to the Son.
Standing in the shadow of the Light,
celebrating him.

I want to be a Life giver
because I am a God gazer.
Not because it's about me
but because it's about him.
Because life can't spring
from any other "thing".

I want to be a World changer
not just a furniture rearranger
or an "it could be better" whinger
or a "have the leftovers" stinger.

I want to be a World changer!
A doer, not just a talker.
I want to spread the clothes of heaven,
no more or less than a poor man's dreams,
beneath the feet of Jesus.

I want to be a World changer
'cos on a morning many winters ago
the tomb was open
and the curse was broken.
Death had to let go
and Recreation burst out
of an old wineskin
like water from a geyser,
like the cry of a Child
pushed into the world,
and nothing
would shut him up.

I want to be a World changer
because it's started...
because the vanguard's on the move...
and Love is pushing out hate
and Light is shining out
and darkness can't understand It,
beat It,
change It,
hide It,
kill It,
stop It,
win.

I want to be a World changer
because there's safety in this danger.
There's meaning in this purpose.
There's joy in this mission
and too many others are missing
the power of life in all its fullness.

World changer? Life giver? God gazer?
God, break in – then break out.
Fill me – then make me leak.
Plug me in and push me out.
In me, through me, around me.
Make me a Patrick!
Make me a Brendan!
God gazing, Life giving, World changing!
Captured by the brilliance
that springs from the radiance
of you!

SECTION ONE

"God Gazers"

A fresh vision of God and a better imagination

Now to him who is able to do immeasurably more than all we ask or imagine, according to his power that is at work within us, to him be glory in the church and in Christ Jesus throughout all generations, for ever and ever! Amen.

Paul's letter to the Ephesians, chapter 3, verses 20–21 (NIV)

Imagination is the voice of daring. If there is anything godlike about God, it is that. He dared to imagine everything.

Henry Miller, Sexus[1]

---

1. Henry Miller, *Sexus: The Rosy Crucifixion*, New York: Grove Press, 1965, Chapter 14.

CHAPTER ONE

I Want to be a God Gazer

I want to be a God gazer!
Captured by the brilliance
that springs from the radiance
of you.

"We would like to see Jesus."

John 12:21 (NIV)

The universe does not revolve around you.

The universe revolves around its Creator. It hangs on his every word. When he speaks, worlds come into being. With every "breath" he holds the planets in their place, and in every second he holds your life in his hands. Without him, you would not be. With him, you are an explosion of life, a part of the Great Story, a person of beauty, significance, and worth. You find your ultimate destiny and purpose and meaning by stepping out of the centre of your own life and giving him the centre stage.

Who's at the centre?

We kid ourselves into thinking that it is all about us, but that is a lie that gets us nowhere.

23

One day, someone else will do the job you do, or something like it. It doesn't matter whether you are the director of a company, the pastor of a church, the chief executive of a charity, a shopkeeper, a nurse, or a doctor. Perhaps the only role we play where that is not true is in our parenting – for those of us who are blessed with children – and in our relationships as children, siblings, and partners. I am challenged by the fact that there are many people who call me "pastor", but only four who can ever call me their dad, two who could call me their son, and four who could call me their sibling.

A generation from now, other bright young things will be taking our place. They will have glittering new ideas and new ways of doing things, they will succeed where we have failed, and they will be the inspiration for their generation. So they should be. They will shine and shimmer in the light of their greatness. They will lead further than you and I have. They will achieve more than you or I thought possible. With guts, determination, and commitment, they will change the world – and so they should. I want to be part of a generation that gives them the chance to be great and to do better than we are doing.

The reality is, though, that with all that they might achieve, they will not be the centres of the world either. That place is reserved for One alone – Almighty God himself. He will not share his centrality with anyone. That decision is not based on selfishness and arrogance; it is based on knowing that with him at the centre of all things, life will be at its most precious and beautiful. The minute we take him out of the centre, things go wrong.

Centrality and discipleship

At the centre of any ideas of Christian discipleship that claim to be biblical in even the remotest sense lies the absolute conviction that our lives revolve around Someone Else.

We are not in the middle of the circle: God is.

There is room at the core of our lives for only one person. Such a space in my life can be occupied by me or by another. God has entrusted to me the decision about who takes that place and whom I invite to sit on that throne. It's my call.

To be a follower of Christ is to give him the throne of our hearts and to follow wherever he leads. When he says jump, we say, "How high?"

Simple.

How big is God?

It was one of our Sunday morning services at Gold Hill and the building was packed. There was hardly room to breathe, let alone move around, and we were about to pray for the children and young people before they left for their own age-specific teaching. I was trying to help the congregation understand the greatness of God.

Looking around at the church family that I love, I asked, "Can anyone tell me how big God is?"

There was the normal laughter and lightness that accompanies our meetings as people responded to one another and a choir of voices answered me in various ways. "Enormous," one child shouted out. "What do you mean?" another child asked.

Then a little boy (I will call him "Josh Hargreaves" to

protect his identity), who I think was about four or five years old at the time, leaned over the balcony and shouted down to me, "He's really big!" There was another roll of laughter and some applause. The congregation was enjoying this dialogue, so I continued with it.

"Is he bigger than me, Josh?" I asked him.

"Of course he is!" Josh shouted down and laughed.

"Is God bigger than your house, Josh?" I continued.

Josh thought for a moment or two, then a huge smile broke across his face, illuminating his eyes and shining out of his heart. "Yup! He's bigger than our house," Josh replied. "He's really, really big!"

"Wow!' I said, as the congregation applauded the little boy's tenacity and precociousness. "Is God bigger than this church, Josh?"

By now Josh was on a roll and he knew exactly what he thought about God. "Yeaahhhhh!" he announced. "He's bigger than EVERYTHING!" and with that he flung his arms wide, as if he were encompassing the entire universe. "God's the biggest that can be!" he yelled, and then he sat down triumphantly.

The congregation cheered, then a strange thing happened. I said, "Exactly, Josh," and I turned to the church family and guests who were present that day and I said, "So why do we worry so much? Why do we make him so small? Why do we keep Him at the edge of our lives so often?"

There was a holy silence.

You could have heard a pin drop.

In just a few simple sentences, that little boy taught us something of the greatness of God that we so often forget.

God is bigger than everything.

God is bigger than we think

We need a fresh vision of God. We need to see his greatness again. We need to be captured by his utter vastness, his immeasurable beauty and power. It is only as we catch a fresh vision of him that we can capture a better vision of our own lives.

So often we get tired in our living. For all the right reasons we end up with all the wrong priorities. Life happens and we get on with it. Bringing up children, getting to the office on time, paying the bills, sorting out ageing parents, planning for our retirement, trying to do our best in work. Without realizing it, the lens through which we view our lives becomes smeared with the reality of actually living. Without us ever meaning it to happen, and almost certainly without any of us doing it deliberately, we allow our vision of God to be reduced according to our lives. We limit his greatness and beauty in direct correlation to the extent of our experiences in life. With the grime of disappointment dirtying the lenses of our faith, we reduce God to a more measurable concept and size and we make him no more than a bigger version of ourselves. We allow our hope for the future to be shaped by the disappointments of the past.

That's a big mistake. God is far bigger than we think.

Lessons in our vision of God from Isaiah

Sometime between 742 BC and 739 BC, King Uzziah of Israel died. Having come to the throne as a young man at the age of sixteen (see 2 Kings 15:2), he reigned for about 52 years before contracting leprosy and dying about a year later. In the year that he died, the prophet Isaiah records this:

> It was in the year King Uzziah died that I saw the Lord.
>
> **Isaiah 6:1a (NLT)**

What follows in the rest of Isaiah 6 is an account in which the prophet is changed and transformed by his vision of God. Isaiah's encounter with the Creator leads to a fresh understanding of God's greatness, power, and holiness:

> It was in the year King Uzziah died that I saw the Lord. He was sitting on a lofty throne, and the train of his robe filled the Temple. Attending him were mighty seraphim, each having six wings. With two wings they covered their faces, with two they covered their feet, and with two they flew. They were calling out to each other,
>
> "Holy, holy, holy is the LORD of Heaven's Armies! The whole earth is filled with his glory!"
>
> Their voices shook the Temple to its foundations, and the entire building was filled with smoke.
>
> **Isaiah 6:1–4 (NLT)**

This leads to Isaiah becoming acutely aware of his own shortcomings and failures and sin:

> Then I said, "It's all over! I am doomed, for I am a sinful man. I have filthy lips, and I live among a people with filthy lips. Yet I have seen the King, the LORD of Heaven's Armies."
>
> **Isaiah 6:5 (NLT)**

As the prophet acknowledges his own weakness, Isaiah receives a fresh touch of cleansing and empowering from God when one of the angels in the vision flies to the prophet from the altar and touches Isaiah's lips with burning coal, cleansing him:

> Then one of the seraphim flew to me with a
> burning coal he had taken from the altar with a
> pair of tongs. He touched my lips with it and said,
> "See, this coal has touched your lips. Now your
> guilt is removed, and your sins are forgiven."
>
> Isaiah 6:6–7 (NLT)

There then follows a call to "go" and to "speak", to which Isaiah responds:

> Then I heard the Lord asking, "Whom should I
> send as a messenger to this people? Who will go
> for us?"
> I said, "Here I am. Send me."
> And he said, "Yes, go, and say to this people…"
>
> Isaiah 6:8–9

In short, Isaiah has a fresh vision of God that leads to a fresh mission for God. In fact, the mission that Isaiah receives is an extremely difficult one. It is outlined in the remainder of Isaiah 6. God tells Isaiah that the people to whom God is sending him will not listen to the prophet. They will not understand what he is saying and they will not obey God's voice through Isaiah.

There is much I could say about the nature of what Isaiah is called to do, but I want to focus on how Isaiah receives this fresh mission from God. Isaiah encounters God afresh before he serves God afresh. He has a fresh glimpse of the greatness, the glory, the holiness, and the beauty of God before he takes up a fresh mission for God.

We need a fresh vision of God before we attempt fresh things for him too. We need to see him as he is before we do what he asks us to do. So often we allow our vision of God to be domesticated, reduced, and limited by our circumstances and the voices around us. Yet God is so much bigger than we think.

Isaiah's fresh vision of God came at a time of sadness, mourning, and national uncertainty for Israel. Just at the moment when circumstances looked darkest, God shone brightest. Isaiah saw God and then saw his circumstances differently. That is the right way round. God met Isaiah right in the middle of life, and God will do the same with us. Our vision of him will shape our vision of ourselves and of our purpose if we let it. Our society needs a fresh hope, a fresh vision, and a fresh purpose, but our society will only have that vision when the people who make up society have a fresh vision out of which they can live.

The Russian Christian and political dissident Aleksandr Solzhenitsyn spent many years in prison during the years of the Soviet Union. In his Templeton Address in 1983, he commented on what had happened to Russia during the time of Communist rule:

> More than half a century ago, while I was still a child, I recall hearing a number of older people offer the following explanation for the great disasters that had befallen Russia: **Men have forgotten God; that's why all this has happened**.

Since then I have spent well-nigh fifty years working on the history of our Revolution; in the process I have read hundreds of books, collected hundreds of personal testimonies, and have already contributed eight volumes of my own toward the effort of clearing away the rubble left by that upheaval. But if I were asked today to formulate as concisely as possible the main cause of the ruinous Revolution that swallowed up some sixty million of our people, I could not put it more accurately than to repeat: **Men have forgotten God; that's why all this has happened.**
What is more, the events of the Russian Revolution can only be understood now, at the end of the century, against the background of what has since occurred in the rest of the world. What emerges here is a process of universal significance. And if I were called upon to identify briefly the principal trait of the entire twentieth century, here too, I would be unable to find anything more precise and pithy than to repeat once again: **Men have forgotten God.**[2]

There is the great challenge – people forgot God. For our lives to have fresh vision and purpose, we need to see God again. Put bluntly, there is no other way. We need to see God again – the real God, not just some blown-up version of us who approves of our choices and baptizes our prejudices. We need a fresh vision of the great, powerful, life-giving, and holy God who met Isaiah. He is our only hope.

---

2 Aleksandr Solzhenitsyn, Templeton Address, 1983 (emphasis added). Used with the permission of Editions Fayard.

Captured by the brilliance

Something happens in a human being's life when God meets them. We are changed. I do not mean we have a brief external renaissance of hope. I mean we are changed. Deep within, something is changed when we truly meet God. A brief glimpse at the stories of the central figures of the Bible show us what happens when we encounter God. Abram and Sarai's encounters with God in Genesis 12–25 led to a change of name, a change of identity, and a change of purpose. As Jacob met and wrestled with God at Peniel, his walk was permanently changed (Genesis 32) and he became "Israel". In Exodus 3, Moses encountered God in a bush that burned but was never consumed. He was fundamentally changed, and he left the safety of his obscurity to lead the Hebrew people out of Egypt. As he wandered through the wilderness, Moses needed to know that God was with him and leading him. Moses refused to go any further until he had a personal encounter with God. To serve God, he needed to encounter God (Exodus 33–34). In the story of Job, this man who suffered a great deal and had heard of God was transformed not only through his suffering but also through his encounter with God. At the end of his great trial, Job declared to God:

> I had heard of you by the hearing of the ear,
> but now my eye sees you;
> therefore I despise myself,
> and repent in dust and ashes.

Job 42:5–6

The apostle Paul was utterly transformed by his personal encounter with the Lord Jesus Christ. Once a Pharisee, a legalist, and a persecutor of Christians, he had held the coats of those who had stoned Stephen, the first Christian martyr (Acts 8:1), yet he was soon completely changed by a direct and personal encounter with the risen Christ (Acts 9). This encounter utterly transformed him, and he referred to it several times during his life and ministry (Acts 22, 26). He was so transformed that he considered everything in his life rubbish compared to the richness of knowing Christ (Philippians 3).

John, the companion and friend of Jesus, spoke movingly of his own encounter with God through Jesus. We cannot read the opening words of his general epistle without realizing just how much Christ changed this man:

> We declare to you what was from the beginning,
> what we have heard, what we have seen with our
> eyes, what we have looked at and touched with our
> hands, concerning the word of life.

1 John 1:1

When the rest of the disciples had met the risen Christ and were trying to help Thomas to understand what had taken place, their exclamation demonstrates the importance of their encounter. "We have seen the Lord!" they cried (John 20:25), but Thomas was clear that he could not believe until he saw the Lord for himself.

Be careful not to settle for knowing facts *about* Jesus Christ and *about* his Father and *about* the Holy Spirit at the expense of actually encountering God *for himself*. Much of the lifelessness of modern Christianity around the world can be explained by the fact that many Christians have lost sight of the importance of a personal relationship *with* God the Father *through* the Lord Jesus Christ *by the power of* the Holy Spirit. No amount of knowledge will ever be enough to replace a direct encounter with God himself, who comes to us that we might know him. After all, he told his people that they would seek him and they would find him, if they sought him with all of their hearts, (Jeremiah 29:13). As they were being dragged into exile, torn away from their homeland and the security of their Temple and their surroundings, God told them that they would still find him if they sought him. Circumstances cannot keep God away from us; only our lack of desire does that.

God is ready, willing, and able to shine the brilliance of his grace into your life. That is not the question.

The question is whether or not you are ready to let him.

CHAPTER TWO

Not a Cheap Food Grazer

I want to be a God gazer!
Not a cheap food grazer
or an easy option lazer.

For God, who said, "Let there be light in the
darkness," has made this light shine in our hearts so
we could know the glory of God that is seen in the
face of Jesus Christ.

2 Corinthians 4:6 (NLT)

Ready meals are so much easier to live on than a healthy and balanced diet. They fit into our lifestyles because they can be bought and stored. We don't have to think about them at all. We bring them home, store them in a freezer, and take them out when we need them. No waiting. No preparing. No complicated instructions. We just take off the cardboard cover, pierce the plastic lid with a fork, pop it into a microwave for a few minutes, and voila! Dinner is ready! The problem is, they aren't good for us and they don't sustain us. A life of ready meals satisfies our immediate need for food, but it doesn't sustain us in the long run. If we live on them, we end up becoming more and more unhealthy and more and more lazy.

If we are not careful, our encounters with God can end up like ready meals. We take what someone else has prepared and we allow that to become our staple diet. Instead of encountering God for ourselves, we let someone else's encounter with God satisfy us. We end up depending on other people's recipes for our nourishment. We are too busy to read the Bible for ourselves so we let other people read it for us. We replace personal reading of the Scriptures with listening to sermons. We are too busy to worship for ourselves so we let someone else do it for us. We spectate in a worship service instead of choosing to engage in worship ourselves. Instead of using our imagination to enter God's great story and purpose for our lives, we limit our engagement with the Holy Spirit to what we can manage, control, and contain. We don't want to go to the trouble of creating time and space to encounter God because it would demand too much of a change in our lifestyles, so we lower our expectations and thereby stunt our imaginations.

The quick fix doesn't work though. Sooner or later we end up hungry for more. We want to go beyond the bland, the boring, and the manageable. In turning our encounters with God into quick fixes and ready meals, we lose out on the wonder and the beauty and the exhilaration that come from discovering new things about God. If we want to move beyond the quick fix we have to learn to use our imaginations again. God gazers realize that our imaginations are a gift from God. God gazers realize that the key to unlocking a new depth and a new health in our relationships with God is our ability to imagine. God gazers love using their imagination!

One of the greatest gifts that God has given you is your imagination. Through it, new worlds and new possibilities are opened up to you. The imagination is one of the fundamentally human aspects of life that separate us from all other created beings. We can harness our imagination for beauty, for art, for creativity, and for self-expression in ways that are quite different from all other living things. Yet we often do not allow our imaginations to paint pictures of God for us from the truths and the realities of whom he is as revealed in the Bible. Maybe that is because we do not want to turn God into a figment of imagination, or maybe it is because we do not want to dream up new ideas about God. I am not suggesting we should dream up new ideas about God at all. I am, however, suggesting that God has given us our imaginations for a purpose, and as we begin to think about him, we will quickly discover that he is the most precious subject of thought and words and conversation. Our imaginations enable us to enter into the reality of who God is and what he is like, despite our personal circumstances. Our imaginations free us to see the truth *beyond* the difficulties of our lives without pretending that these difficulties are not present. God invites us to encounter him, to think about him, to meditate on him, to dwell on him, to set our hearts on him. As we do so, we see a powerful God who is also a loving and gracious God. We see the Great God and the Near God. We see the God who is here.

The failure to imagine God and to dwell on him and think about him is an easy option. It abdicates our responsibility to think. It trades intimacy for convenience and it diminishes discovery from a journey of possibility to a road trip into the mundane. When we fail to use our imaginations, we confine God to the cell of what we know. God is not simply a construct of our imagination, but when we allow our imaginations to be imprisoned by our circumstances, we also confine our capacity to capture a bigger vision of God. We opt for easy food instead of the bountiful fare of God's presence. We become lazy, and we seek God only for what he can do for us rather than seeking him for who he is.

Our materialistic infatuation with possessions and things and our hedonistic grasps at self-justification have created a world that is far smaller (and far drearier) than the world painted by Scripture. At the same time, our obsession with our own centrality projects a vision of a God who has been denuded of his greatness by Western rationalism, stripped of his personhood by Eastern mysticism, and blindfolded with the dirty rags of scant cultural relativism, and whose voice has been muted because we have stuffed the unwashed sock of political correctness and religious pluralism into his mouth. As a result, many pastors and congregations worship a God who is nothing more than a bigger version of themselves.

It's easier to make God a big version of ourselves than to discover him for who he actually is – wholly other and indescribably beautiful. No surprise, then, that a God who is fashioned by laziness and contained by our infatuation with immediacy cannot deliver us from our plight. We have disabled him. To hide this fact, we engage in what can only be described as an ever-quickening slide into an ever-tightening circle of lifeless and futile religious exercises. God may have left the building, but that doesn't matter because we'd rather stay the same without him than face the inconvenience of being changed by him. The tragedy is that often we'd rather keep the real God out because he is disruptive, untameable, and gloriously free of the constraints of our unimaginative portrayals of him, than risk the consequences of encountering him afresh. Better to keep God small and manageable than allow him to be big and demanding.

The chains of our small understanding of God are broken not by our own effort, but by a fresh encounter with him. It is as we see him as he truly is that our small and confining visions of him are enlarged. There is no profound formula to be learnt here, no recitation of words that will call down God's glory and power into our lives. What limits our encounter with God is our lack of imagination. It is because we cannot cope with who he truly is that we so often miss his greatness. After all, it's far easier to domesticate God and keep him on a leash than it is to pursue him. To pursue him demands effort; to leash him demands control.

He wants to be found by us but he won't force himself on us

The wonder of the thing is that God wants to be found by us. He has always wanted to be found by us. It is why he made us. Augustine said of God, "Thou awakest us to delight in Thy praise; for Thou madest us for Thyself, and our heart is restless, until it repose in Thee. Grant me, Lord, to know and understand which is first, to call on Thee or to praise Thee?"[3] True rest, true meaning, and true purpose come from God and God alone. To discover God

---

3   Edward B. Pussey (trans), *The Confessions of Augustine*, New York: Collier Books, 1961, Book 1, Chapter 1, Page 11.

as he is, however, demands a bit of effort on our part. We cannot just flick open a Bible and point to a random verse. We need to develop a habit of pursuit.

Our imagination is like a muscle. We have to learn to use it, to exercise it, to strengthen it. We have to learn to liberate it from the chains of easy answers and narrow-minded certainty. You cannot simultaneously contain God and pursue him. If we want to see him in new ways, we have to learn to look at him from different angles, and that demands discipline, effort, and intentionality. You won't dig diamonds out of the ground with a toothpick. If you want to unearth a diamond, you have to be willing to dig.

God wants to reveal his greatness and his glory to us. He has never wanted his people to live with a stunted vision of himself. It is our inability to cope with who he is or our unwillingness to genuinely look at him that determines how we see him. We don't see him as he is because we can't cope with who he is. To see him as he is demands a willingness to respond to who he is, and we are often too comfortable with what we know to embark on a new adventure. An encounter with God as he is reveals our nakedness as well as his beauty. To see him as he is makes us realize how much he loves us, but it also causes us to blush at our own laziness and lack of imagination. It has ever been thus since the first stories of creation were told. Adam and Eve "hid" from God because of their sin (Genesis 3:8–10). Cain left the presence of God because he murdered Abel (Genesis 4:9–16). Yet God talked with Noah like a friend because of Noah's openness and faithfulness (Genesis 6:13), as he did with Abraham (Genesis 12:1,7; 13:14; 17:1–3), and he did the same with Moses:

> Thus the LORD used to speak to Moses face to face,
> as one speaks to a friend.
>
> **Exodus 33:11**

God wanted the kind of intimate and personal relationship that he had with Moses, Noah, and Abraham, and with Adam, Eve, and Cain (before their shame disrupted it), with all of Israel, but it was Israel that could not cope with such intimacy. Listen to the words of Moses:

> The LORD spoke with you face to face at the
> mountain, out of the fire. (At that time I was
> standing between the LORD and you to declare
> to you the words of the LORD; for you were
> afraid because of the fire and did not go up the
> mountain.)
>
> **Deuteronomy 5:4–5**

> When all the people witnessed the thunder and
> lightning, the sound of the trumpet, and the
> mountain smoking, they were afraid and trembled
> and stood at a distance, and said to Moses, "You
> speak to us, and we will listen; but do not let God
> speak to us, or we will die." Moses said to the
> people, "Do not be afraid; for God has come only
> to test you and to put the fear of him upon you
> so that you do not sin." Then the people stood at
> a distance, while Moses drew near to the thick
> darkness where God was.
>
> **Exodus 20:18–21**

From that moment on, God gave Israel what they wanted. He spoke to them *through* prophets and leaders because they could not cope with him speaking to them in direct and close personal relationship, but it was his desire to be their friend and to be intimate with them. That is still his desire today. He wants to relate to us. He wants us to find him. We, like the Israelites, prefer to relate to him through others because we, like them, are marred by our own fallen nature.

God is not running away from us. He is not playing some of kind of malicious spiritual hide-and-seek. He longs to be encountered by us. He longs to befriend us. I would go as far as to say he misses our company. He not only loves us; he also likes us. It is we who do not love or like him. That is why we hide from him.

How do we hide from him?

It is no more possible to hide from God than it is to defy the ageing process. We can use as many creams, ointments, treatments, vitamins, or compounds as we like, but we cannot avoid getting older. Gravity beats surgery – eventually!

We may be able to fool ourselves into thinking that God is not watching, but we cannot talk ourselves out of the reality of God's presence. We cannot hide somewhere where he is not (Psalm 139 shows us that). There is no place that we can "be" where he is not also present. So instead of fooling ourselves into thinking that we can run *away from* him, what about the idea of running *into* him?

An invitation to intimacy

Intimacy with God is not something that he withholds; it is something we refuse. And it is this refusal that is dealt with through his Son, the new Moses, who not only tells us what God says, but also shows us what God is like. We see his brilliance shine through in the story of the transfiguration of the Lord Jesus. In the account recorded in Mark 9, Jesus took Peter, James, and John to a mountain and there revealed his true nature to them. As they gazed on the transfigured Christ and watched him talking with Elijah and Moses, we read:

> Peter exclaimed, "Rabbi, it's wonderful for us to be here! Let's make three shelters as memorials – one for you, one for Moses, and one for Elijah." He said this because he didn't really know what else to say, for they were all terrified.
>
> **Mark 9:5 (NLT)**

A dark cloud overshadowed them and they heard a voice from the cloud saying:

> "This is my dearly loved Son. Listen to him."
>
> **Mark 9:7 (NLT)**

God longs to lead us to a place where we, too, can see him as he really is. The New Testament shows us clearly that if we want to see what God is really like, we simply need to look at Jesus:

> "Whoever has seen me has seen the Father."
>
> **John 14:9 (ESV)**

Christ, who is the image of God.

2 Corinthians 4:4 (ESV)

He is the image of the invisible God … he is before all things, and in him all things hold together … in him all the fullness of God was pleased to dwell.

Colossians 1:15, 17, 19 (ESV)

He is the radiance of the glory of God and the exact imprint of his nature, and he upholds the universe by the word of his power.

Hebrews 1:3 (ESV)

Isaiah saw the Lord "high and lifted up" in the Temple in Jerusalem. We, every single one of us, are invited to "see the Lord" in the person, work, and ministry of Jesus Christ. It is in Jesus Christ that we see the radiance of the brilliance of God.

Jesus is not just a good moral example, although he is surely that. He is not just a teacher of high calibre and wise words, although he is that too. He is not one of a number of options from which we can choose. Jesus of Nazareth is God enrobed in flesh. If we want to see what God is really like, we start with Christ.

We see God's brilliance in the radiance of Christ's face.

Hebrew philosophy idealized light, seeing it as the epitome of truth and life and hailing it as the great pursuit of their culture. That is why they could say that the Lord was their light and their salvation (Psalm 27:1), or that those who had walked in darkness would see great light (Isaiah 9:2). The Greeks yearned for knowledge, which is why John said he had written his Gospel – so that his

44

readers might believe and have eternal life (John 20:31). The Romans yearned for glory. So it is not surprising that Paul, a *Roman* citizen who was *Hebrew* by birth and lived in a *Greek* city, set out his ideal, his highest thought and noblest truth about Jesus, and in so doing captured the brilliance of the Hebrews, the Greeks, and the Romans. For Paul, it was simple – Christ captures it all:

> For we do not proclaim ourselves; we proclaim Jesus Christ as Lord and ourselves as your slaves for Jesus' sake. For it is the God who said, "Let **light** shine out of darkness," who has shone in our hearts to give **the light of the knowledge of the glory of God in the face of Jesus Christ**.
>
> **2 Corinthians 4:5–6 (emphasis added)**

The ultimate expression of life, beauty, meaning, and purpose is not an idea or an ideal; it is a Person. Light, knowledge, and glory converge in one place. We see the splendour and depth and brilliant radiance of God *in the face of Jesus Christ*.

An invitation to encounter

It strikes me that here is one of the simplest and yet most overlooked invitations to see what God is like. Simply pick up a New Testament and read of the works, words, and attitudes of Jesus, the Son of God. His brilliance leaks through every page; his radiance permeates every word, every syllable, and every phrase. In him we see the compassion of God for those of us who feel useless and weak. In him we see hope in human form as he lifts the fallen, forgives the guilty, restores the tarnished, and redeems the enslaved. In him the lost find a Way. In him the liars find the Truth. In him the dead find Life. His words are like torches that set fire to the lies that tell us that we do not matter and that God does not care. His actions illuminate the life of every human being and show us what it means to be truly alive. He is the power supply that never runs out, the Son that will never set. His grace and love and acceptance are the eternal dawn, which rises always in our hearts and brings with it healing, hope, and peace. Our church services can no more contain him than a thimble can contain an ocean. Our music can no more convey his grandeur than a child's plastic toy can convey a symphony. Our words can no more describe him than a dictionary can help us capture the heartbeat of love.

No. We must encounter him if we are to see him. It is only in relationship that increasing revelation is possible. Before we can be captured by his brilliance, there must be an unlocking of our hearts, an opening up of the possibility of a love relationship. Devotion and revelation walk hand in hand.

The only thing that can capture who he is for us is meeting him. Seeing him. Witnessing him. Encountering him. Our best efforts are nothing more than faltering and stammering introductions to the most beautiful, most glorious, most wonderful person. There comes a point when the introductions are over and the chaperone must leave so that the lover and the loved can be alone.

Encountering God through Jesus means that we must make the effort to read about him. The Bible will remain a locked store for us if we do not read it. There is a huge wave of biblical illiteracy sweeping the church around the world, and we must resist it. We are raising a generation of Christians whose knowledge of Christ is shaped by other people's books and other people's sermons. They are surviving on meagre servings of food given to them from a tiny spoon each Sunday morning in church. Their Bibles are closed for six days of the week. The ensuing chasm of understanding and knowledge is then filled by people who present a cheap and easy Jesus. Our problem is that we are seeing leaders emerge into God's church who are presenting the Jesus that they like rather than the Jesus of the Scriptures. We end up with fast-food religion, easy spirituality, and distorted images of what Jesus is like and therefore of what God is like.

We have allowed the culture to shape Jesus instead of allowing the Jesus of the Bible to shape the culture. He has become a bland Saviour. He gives us what we want, he makes us feel good about ourselves, and he never expects us to change. This is a far cry from the Jesus of the Bible. His beauty is breathtaking because he is utterly forgiving and yet utterly unyielding. His grace does not mean we can do what we like; his grace means we can live a better way (Matthew 5).

Jesus doesn't dismiss the demands of a Holy God; he fulfils them. He comforts the troubled and troubles the comfortable. He asks us for the whole of our lives. He challenges our assumptions, he breaks our prejudices, and he reminds us of our desperate need of a Saviour. He carries the punishment we deserve and he absorbs the wrath of God on our behalf. He takes what we deserve (punishment) and he gives us what we do not deserve (forgiveness and hope). His sacrifice pronounces us righteous – legally, forensically, and forever – and he demands all of our lives. He gives his all to us and asks our all from us. He defends us and challenges us. He forgives us and fashions us. He embraces us and he disciplines us. His depth and beauty and power and holiness take our breath away. He is indescribable.

It is only when you are left speechless that you will truly know you have met the Word who lives forever. He is not just a reason for living: he is all our reasons, and once you have seen him, nothing that anyone can ever offer you will compare to the brilliance that springs from his radiance.

He is, after all, the Light of the world.

We need to "see Jesus" again

We must be careful not to turn Christianity into nothing more than a learned faith. It cannot simply be "discovered" intellectually. A person is not converted just because they assent to a set of doctrines and beliefs and practices. Christianity is a *revealed* faith. It is not enough simply to be rationally persuaded, although that is of great importance. Christians are people who have been *captured by the brilliance that springs from the radiance* of God himself.

At this point I must confess that I have never *seen* Jesus. Unlike all those people from the Bible I have mentioned, I have never *seen* God in a literal sense. "Well then, Malcolm," you might argue, "you are contradicting yourself. How can you say that we need an encounter with God before we discover a fresh mission for God if you have never *seen* Jesus?" The answer is simple: while I have never *seen* Jesus in the flesh and while I have never *seen* God in the flesh, I have seen him in the lives of millions of Christians, and I have seen him in the pages of the Bible.

The Scriptures paint such a strong picture of what God is like that it is as if he is standing before us, Luther once argued. If we want to be captured by the brilliance of God, we allow the stories, the events, and the truths of the Bible to come alive in our hearts and in our minds. Indeed, in Jesus we see exactly what God is like because Jesus is the *reflection of God's glory and the exact imprint of God's very being* (Hebrews 1:3). Jesus is the one in whom the fullness of God dwells in bodily form:

> He is the image of the invisible God, the firstborn of all creation; for in him all things in heaven and on earth were created, things visible and invisible, whether thrones or dominions or rulers or powers – all things have been created through him and for him. He himself is before all things, and in him all things hold together. He is the head of the body, the church; he is the beginning, the firstborn from the dead, so that he might come to have first place in everything. For in him all the fullness of God was pleased to dwell, and through him God was pleased to reconcile to himself all things, whether on earth or in heaven, by making peace through the blood of his cross.
>
> **Colossians 1:15–20**

So you see, I may not have *seen* Jesus in the flesh, and I may not have *seen* God in the literal sense that Isaiah did in the year that King Uzziah died, but I have seen him. I have seen him in the person and ministry of Jesus. I have seen him in the events and encounters of the Bible. I have seen him in the lives of men and women around the world who have surrendered their lives to him. I have seen him in the great story of the church down through the years. I do not need to *see* him in the flesh to *see* him through the eyes of faith, because I have come to believe in Jesus.

Did you notice what I said? I did not say that I simply believe *about* Jesus. I said I have come to believe *in* Jesus. There is a world of difference between these two statements. One is able to recount facts about God; the other is able to describe God as Companion, Friend, Saviour, and Lord.

As you read these words, God is present beside you. Do you want to know what he is like? Pick up a Bible and read one of the Gospels. If you are interested in Jesus the Jew, read Matthew. If you are interested in Jesus the kingdom-bringer and the swift-footed Saviour, read Mark. If you are interested in Jesus who brings the power of his Spirit to us and transforms us, read Luke. If you are interested in Jesus the ultimate source of light and life and hope, read John. Jesus is ready to capture your imagination and feed your soul.

He wants you to see him now. He's right there beside you as you read these words. He's waiting for you to look at him. He is where he has always been. The question is not whether he wants to reveal himself to you; the question is whether you dare look at him – because once you do, you'll never be the same again.

When you see him, your response will be the same as Isaiah's was. You will have the same response as Peter, James, and John. You will see his beauty and greatness and immediately feel your own smallness and become aware of your own shortcomings and failings. Do not be dismayed, though, because as you acknowledge your smallness, he comes to cleanse and renew and refresh you. A great change takes place in our lives when we truly encounter God.

A God gazer knows that they can never be the same again once they have allowed God to use their imagination. We'll never be contained by our situations because God is bigger than anything we face and anything we experience. We do not want to be trapped within an imagination that has shrivelled. We will not let someone who has given up on their dream persuade us to give up on ours. We want to see God more clearly than we have ever seen him. We want to know him better. We want to see him in fresh and new ways.

To truly see him, however, to truly look at him, takes courage and a willingness to be changed. It is a daring and adventurous thing to do.

I dare you – look at him.

Really look at him.

Slow down and intentionally look at him.

When you do, you will discover that he is always looking at you.

CHAPTER THREE

Trailblazers for the Ordinary Life

I want to be a trailblazer
for the ordinary, everyday life.

"Give your entire attention to what God is doing
right now, and don't get worked up about what may
or may not happen tomorrow. God will help you
deal with whatever hard things come up when the
time comes."

The Lord Jesus Christ, Matthew 6:34 (The Message)

It's when I get lost in the day's details, or so caught
up in worries about what might be, that I miss the
beauty of what is.

Katrina Kenison, The Gift of an Ordinary Day: A Mother's Memoir

B eing ordinary is a beautiful thing, and we should celebrate it a great deal more. Christians and local churches are not always very good at celebrating ordinariness. I'm not entirely sure why that is, but I have my ideas. Maybe we sometimes get stuck in a rut in our lives and we long for something more exciting, more unpredictable, to spice things up a bit. There's nothing wrong with that. Maybe we like to have a superstar to point to, someone we can look up to and aspire to be like. There is nothing wrong with that either. Maybe we have been taught that God moves miraculously today and that Christ's body, the church, is a community where the power of the gospel is demonstrated in healing and in supernatural power. There is nothing wrong with that either.

Maybe we long for something else because we think we are not good enough, or we think that God cannot do anything with our ordinary lives unless we change them. There is something very wrong with that. Maybe we think that God can only use the men and women on platforms, the big names, the well-known preachers and teachers. There is something very wrong with that. Maybe we never hear anything in church about our everyday lives and therefore we assume that they don't matter. There is something very wrong with that. Maybe we think that the only thing we should do once we become Christians is attend meetings, bring people to church services, and see our careers and our everyday lives as fishing grounds for converts. There is something very wrong with that.

The fear of ordinariness

If we are not careful, we can end up with a fear of ordinariness. We can fear it in our everyday life, we can fear it in our family and our career, we can fear it in our relationship with God, and we can fear it in our church. I think that is partly a cultural thing – the world around us is obsessed with celebrity and with glitz and with glamour so there is bound to be an impact on the church and on the way Christians think. I also think our fear of ordinariness can be fuelled by a wrong understanding of Christian spirituality.

Let me address the issue of ordinariness by first looking at three ideas. Those ideas are yearning for God (which is good), striving after God (which is not good), and kingdom thinking (which is vital if we are to keep a right perspective).

Yearning

There is a good kind of yearning after God and a bad kind of yearning after God. The good kind is the kind that the Bible speaks of. For example, in our quest for greater intimacy with God we are taught to hunger and thirst after righteousness: Jesus taught his disciples that those who hungered after God in such a way would be filled (Matthew 5:6), and we are told that those who seek the Lord will lack no good thing (Psalm 34:10). Indeed, I have already encouraged you to seek the Lord because you will find him when you seek him with all your heart (Jeremiah 29:13). There is a yearning and a longing after God which is a gift that is given to us by God. We hear it echoed in the words of King David:

> The LORD *is* my light and my salvation;
> Whom shall I fear?
> The LORD *is* the strength of my life;
> Of whom shall I be afraid? …
> One *thing* have I desired of the LORD,

That will I seek:
That I may dwell in the house of the LORD
All the days of my life,
To behold the beauty of the LORD,
And to inquire in His temple …
Hear, O LORD, *when* I cry with my voice!
Have mercy also upon me, and answer me.
When You said, "Seek My face,"
My heart said to You, "Your face, LORD, I will seek"…
Wait on the LORD;
Be of good courage,
And He shall strengthen your heart;
Wait, I say, on the LORD!

Psalm 27:1, 4, 7, 8, 14 (NKJV)

This is the yearning captured by Paul's words to the Philippians, that he was straining forward to take hold of everything that Christ had made him to be (Philippians 3). Even as an old man, Paul could write to Timothy and speak of his continued longing after God (2 Timothy 4). This is a good yearning. It is a longing to grow in God, to develop a greater intimacy with and a greater knowledge of God. It is a desire to see God's kingdom demonstrated and evidenced in our world today. Jesus taught us that such an attitude was right. He taught us to pray that God's kingdom would come on earth as it is in heaven (Luke 11), and he instructed his disciples to heal the sick, raise the dead, and cast out demons (Matthew 10, 12, 28; Mark 16).

Such hungering and thirsting after the power of God in our lives is right and good and proper. A daily yearning to be being filled with the Holy Spirit should be one of the distinctive characteristics of the Christian's life (Ephesians 5:18).

The passage of Scripture that shows me this yearning most movingly is the wonderful book of Song of Songs. Originally written as a love song to celebrate human intimacy and love between a man and a woman, the book is also rich in images and overtones that can be applied to the relationship between the church as Christ's bride and Christ as our lover:

> While I slept, my heart was awake.
> I dreamed my lover knocked at the door.
>
> Let me come in, my darling,
> my sweetheart, my dove.
> My head is wet with dew,
> and my hair is damp from the mist.
>
> I have already undressed;
> why should I get dressed again?
> I have washed my feet;
> why should I get them dirty again?
>
> My lover put his hand to the door,
> and I was thrilled that he was near.
> I was ready to let him come in.
> My hands were covered with myrrh,
> my fingers with liquid myrrh,
> as I grasped the handle of the door.
> I opened the door for my lover,
> but he had already gone.
> How I wanted to hear his voice!

> I looked for him, but couldn't find him;
> I called to him, but heard no answer.

Song of Songs 5:2–6 (Good News Translation)

Such yearning for more intimacy and more revelation of who God is and what he is like is a beautiful thing. A longing that yearns for God to move more powerfully in our lives and in our communities is right, and from it springs greater intimacy and a greater sense of walking in God's ways, as well as a greater delight and joy in our salvation.

Striving

Yearning brings life and vitality and hope and wholeness. Striving, on the other hand, brings desperation and fear and anxiety and brokenness. Paul told Timothy that godliness with contentment brings great gain (1 Timothy 6:6), and the psalmist said that those who look to the Lord are radiant (Psalm 34:5). Yet the Bible warns against a hard sense of being driven. Rather than striving after a God we cannot reach, we are invited to become aware of a God who is closer to us than we could ever dream of or hope.

God is nearer than we think. The invitation of Psalm 46 to "Be still and know that I am God" could be equally well translated, "Stop striving," or "Stop trying so hard," or even "Lay down your arms." We are reminded that in quietness and confidence shall be our strength. Perhaps the most memorable words of the Bible are those contained in Psalm 23 that remind us that because the Lord is our shepherd, we have everything we need. Jesus told his disciples not to be anxious about what tomorrow would bring (Matthew 6), and Paul told the Philippians not to be anxious about anything but instead to trust God (Philippians 4:6).

Striving is what happens when we become so discontented with where we are that we become critical, negative, impatient, or untrusting. Yearning is an expression of trust and hope, but striving is an expression of discontent and deep unhappiness. Striving is about trying too hard, about relying on one's own strength or ability. Yearning is about seeking after God.

The great challenge of striving is that we become discontented with everything eventually. We never feel that we have enough of God. We never feel that we have progressed enough in our careers. We become so focused on the *next* thing that we cannot enjoy the present thing. Even in the midst of seeing God doing wonderful things in our lives and in our churches, we become desperate for him to do more. The result is a disquieted spirit and a deep feeling that somehow we will never be happy.

Kingdom thinking

I admit that there can be a fine line between yearning and striving. The desire to grow in God is vital to a healthy Christian life, and it helps us avoid complacency. Being continually impatient with ourselves, with God, and with others is a dangerous trait for Christians. It can lead to spiritual superiority and aloofness on the one hand and a deep sense of discontent on the other. A core way of working out whether we are yearning or striving is the way in which we understand the kingdom of God.

Many in the church today have given up hope of seeing

the kingdom come in power. This is a deep tragedy and it leads to spiritual apathy and cynicism. Those who have fallen prey to this malaise are cynical and cold-hearted. They have lost their joy and the excitement of following Christ. They are the people who are always ready to tell you why something cannot work.

Others, however, have fallen into the trap of thinking that absolutely everything that Christ has promised to his people should happen now. They want to see every church service as a summary of the book of Acts. Unless God moves in healing power and the worship hits new heights and the preaching is off the scale every week, they are disappointed. They want all people everywhere to be healed immediately. They teach that suffering and poverty and sorrow are not part of the Christian's life and that we should reject any notion of such things. They will even use phrases that sound very plausible, suggesting that we should not allow the level of our theology to be shaped by the level of our experience.

That all sounds great, but there are a couple of problems with it. Firstly, Jesus never promised us this kind of life. Secondly, God never speaks to us from a vacuum, and he never speaks to us in a vacuum. Our faith is always worked out in the everyday events of our lives. If it does not make sense there, then it will not make sense anywhere. Thirdly, if we are waiting on God changing something before we can be content or at peace in him, then we will never be content or at peace in him. If we cannot encounter him where we are, we will never encounter him somewhere else.

The power of ordinary lives submitted to God

The church has always had leading lights. These lights may have been people like the apostles or the early church fathers and mothers such as Augustine, Gregory, Amma Sarah, or Theodora. God has raised up people like Luther, Calvin, the Wesleys, and Whitfield. He has give us people like the Earl of Shaftesbury. He has given the church pioneers like William and Catherine Booth, Selina the Countess of Huntingdon, and Elizabeth Fry. More recently, we should thank God for men and women with extraordinary gifts in preaching and teaching and encouragement such as John Stott, Martin Lloyd-Jones, Jackie Pullinger, Pope Francis, Billy and Ruth Graham, Catherine Marshall, and Elizabeth Elliot. People such as Rolland and Heidi Baker are making a massive difference in the world. The Bakers' ministry in Mozambique is providing hope and support to many children. Barnabas Mam in Cambodia is planting churches and being used by God to bring hope to many. Simon Guillebaud is making a significant difference in Burundi. I could name many people whose ordinary lives shine out the grace and hope of God. I am sure you could too. Not only that, but God has also given the church extraordinary moves of his Spirit.

Great revivals down through history or great waves of healing and renewal have swept countless thousands into the kingdom of God. The two Great Awakenings, the Irish Revivals, the Welsh Revival, the Hebridean Revival, the outpourings in Azuza Street at the turn of the twentieth century, and many more localized revivals and renewals have strengthened the church and encouraged the saints. Great leaders and great episodes in the life of the church have brought freedom, hope, and purpose to countless Christians. My prayer is that God would continue to do such things and that we would see many powerful moves of the Holy Spirit in the life of the church in the years that lie ahead.

A problem arises, however, when we view our ordinary lives as somehow inferior to the lives of such great leaders, or when we see the ordinary, everyday life of the church as somehow less than central to the purposes of God. None of the men and women I have mentioned set out to be superstars. None of the revivals or renewals I have cited began with the view that they would "go global". They were all, every last one of them, ordinary men and women and ordinary churches and communities who simply allowed the Lord to do what he wanted to do through them.

We must be very careful to avoid the temptation of looking to the latest great preacher or the latest great revival to be the person or the thing that will bring God's kingdom crashing in upon us. I can understand the temptation to pin our hopes on such individuals or such moves of the Spirit. After all, when Jesus was transfigured before Peter, John, and James, Peter wanted them all to stay on the mountaintop for ever (Mark 9). It is a natural tendency to try and enshrine a special moment or enthrone a special teacher or leader. Jesus does not want us to do this, however, because he knows that it is in our everyday lives that we shine most brightly.

I believe in the miraculous, healing, and delivering power of Jesus. I pray for the sick regularly in the contexts where I minister. Our church family has an expectation that God moves when his people meet. However, we also recognize that our everyday lives matter deeply to God.

They are not second-best alternatives to the power of the Holy Spirit. Our everyday lives are the context in which God moves – the way we treat one another, the way we handle our finances, the way we go about our business, and the way we behave in work. These are all acts of worship and devotion to Jesus. They are not the unexciting bits of our lives. They are the powerful moment-by-moment situations in which God speaks to those around us.

The book of Acts was not meant to happen in every church service. The idea that a good meeting must always reach new heights in worship, bring deeper revelation of who God is, and see at least one person saved, one person healed, and one person delivered is not only unbiblical; it is damaging. It damages the ordinary lives of saints who choose to make a daily choice to put Jesus first. It damages the biblical truth that every person's work and calling is holy and important. It promotes a sacred–secular divide that is not only unhelpful but is also deeply detrimental to the kingdom of God. It skews discipleship. It presents an unhealthy picture of Christian living and places heavy burdens on people of man-made expectations that are impossible to meet. It neutralizes the power of ordinary living.

Your ordinary life is the place where God has planted you

Every one of us has a God-given part to play in the manifestation of his kingdom on the earth. Whether we are single, married, or divorced. Whatever our background, whatever our jobs, wherever we are placed by God, we can shine for him. The key lies in understanding that in our ordinary lives, the beautiful light of Christ can shine out from us if we let it.

There is no such thing as an *ordinary* life. Each one of us is created by God, made in his image (Genesis 1:26–28), and each one of us has been given wonderful gifts, skills, and characteristics through which God can display his splendour. Every Christian is a masterpiece of God's design (Ephesians 2:10). It is as we understand this reality that we can shine for him more brightly. Paul captured this remarkable truth in several of the letters that he wrote to the early church. At the heart of his understanding of obedience, worship, and discipleship lies this basic principle of letting God shine out of our daily lives:

> Let the peace of Christ keep you in tune with each other, in step with each other. None of this going off and doing your own thing. And cultivate thankfulness. Let the Word of Christ – the Message – have the run of the house. Give it plenty of room in your lives. Instruct and direct one another using good common sense. And sing, sing your hearts out to God! **Let every detail in your lives – words, actions, whatever – be done in the name of the Master, Jesus, thanking God the Father every step of the way.**
>
> **Colossians 3:15–17 (The Message, emphasis added)**

So here's what I want you to do. God helping you: Take your everyday, ordinary life – your sleeping, eating, going-to-work and walking-around life – and place it before God as an offering. Embracing what God does for you is the best thing you can do for him. Don't become so well-adjusted to your culture that you fit into it without even thinking. Instead, fix your attention on God. You'll be changed from the inside out. Readily recognize what he wants from you, and quickly respond to it. Unlike the culture around you, always dragging you down to its level of immaturity, God brings the best out of you, develops well-formed maturity in you.

Romans 12:1–3 (The Message)

The ordinariness of our lives is not a curse; it is a gift. When we see our daily circumstances as those *into which* God has placed us, we are given a fresh, new sense of value and confidence in what we do. It is as we see our daily circumstances as opportunities for ministry and service of Christ that we are able to shine out God's colours of hope and life into the world around us and bring the flavours of grace, forgiveness, and truth to the world (Matthew 5:13–14, *The Message*).

I have led churches for more than twenty years, and I have come to realize that it is the unknown men and women who have built God's kingdom down through the years. In one of the churches that I led, called Mortimer West End Chapel, the building was constructed in 1798. On the outside wall of the building, men and women had carved their initials into the bricks. I have no idea who they were, but they helped to build God's kingdom, and their sacrifice means that our generation has a building to use and resources to share for the glory of God.

The church I currently lead, Gold Hill, is made up of around 1,000 people who together are making a difference for the kingdom. They get up and go to work every day. They bring up their children. They pray, they give, they worship. They read their Bibles. They volunteer in youth clubs and they run beach missions. They are directors of companies, teachers, nurses, doctors, surgeons, shopkeepers, clerks, factory workers, and farmers. They run small groups. They commute to London. They look after ageing parents. They are good neighbours. They give financially to the work of Gold Hill and a thousand other things. They aren't perfect, because none of us is perfect. They have their fears and their worries and their questions, just as you and I do. Yet their ordinary lives display God's beauty.

We aren't all called to be pastors, teachers, evangelists, prophets, or apostles, but we are all called. We aren't all called to be preachers, but we are all called to be able to give an answer for the hope we have. We aren't all called to stand on platforms, but we have all been given a platform in our daily life. We don't all lead churches, but we all lead someone.

For some of you reading these words, it is enough that you are still serving Jesus. You have felt like a second-class Christian for long enough. Your ordinary, everyday life is of deep significance to God. In fact, your everyday life is so important that Paul connects your daily relationships to the giving of the Holy Spirit more often than he connects the Holy Spirit to miracles and gifts. Your ordinary life is a thing of dazzling beauty and eternal significance. As you sit at your desk tomorrow, or walk into the shop, the factory, or the farm, or pick up your books in the classroom, you do so as a member of God's family. Even if you never see a miracle (and I pray you do), remember that your life is a miracle of God's grace.

God gazers know that God is with them right where they are. They don't need their situation to change before they serve God because they have discovered the earth-shattering truth that God can change the situations around us *through* us. They don't want to be somewhere else; they want to be wherever God wants them to be.

May you be given the grace, the power, and the freedom to shine right where you are, because where you are, God is. That's right. Where you are, God is. God is where you are. Shine out Sister. Shine out Brother. You are his light.

CHAPTER FOUR

Beyond the Halcyon Ways

I want to be a God gazer!
Not just copying the halcyon ways
that shimmer brighter in the haze
of bygone rays and the good old days.

Grow old along with me!
The best is yet to be,
The last of life, for which the first was made:
Our times are in His hand
Who saith "A whole I planned,
Youth shows but half; trust God: see all, nor
*   be afraid!"*

Robert Browning, "Rabbi Ben Ezra"

S omething very strange happened to me in the couple of weeks that followed my decision to follow Christ. Two incidents took place, separated by a week, that left a deep impression on me. Both incidents involved an older person who had been a Christian much longer than I had. One showed me what I did not want my attitude to life to be like, and the other showed me what I wanted my attitude to life to be like.

The first incident took place around three weeks after I was converted, in 1986. When I became a Christian, I immediately had a great hunger for God. It was like someone had turned on a switch in my head. I was given a ferocious appetite for reading the Bible. Given that I had never read the Bible before, this passionate yearning to read the Scriptures surprised me. I remember going home and telling my parents that I had become a Christian, then finding an old illustrated Bible that my sister had bought me years earlier as a birthday present (I resented the present at the time: what eight- or nine-year-old wants a Bible as a birthday present?!) and beginning to read it. I was absolutely gripped! I started at the beginning of the New Testament and read the whole way through in just three days. Within a week, I had read the whole Bible. I loved it. I couldn't believe what I was reading.

I saw Jesus in a way I had never ever thought I would. He spoke the truth, healed the sick, raised the dead, and confronted the self-righteous. He accepted people like me – people who didn't think they were worth very much. He called ordinary people to follow him. He built his church on the foundations of ordinary fishermen. He suffered and died for me. He took the punishment that I deserved. His sacrifice meant that God the Father declared me righteous. Jesus paid for my sin and his Father gave me what I didn't deserve – forgiveness and justification. It was amazing!

Once I had started reading the Bible, I just kept reading it. To be honest, that was nearly thirty years ago and I still love the Bible. I don't read it through in a week very often now, but I do still read it from cover to cover three or four times a year.

News of this young man who had become a Christian and was passionate about reading the Bible spread into the local church where I was converted, and people were intrigued by it. One Sunday evening, about three weeks after my conversion, an elderly lady approached me after the service. She asked me if I was the young man who had become a Christian a few weeks before. I said I was. She commented that I seemed to be very excited and passionate about my newly found faith. I said I was, and I talked a little about my newfound enjoyment of reading the Bible and attending church and prayer and worship and so on. Then she looked me straight in the eye and said something I will never forget: "Oh, don't worry son, that'll soon pass! I was like that once too, but I've settled down!"

I couldn't believe it! Here I was, a new Christian, enjoying all the delights and excitements of the Christian faith and falling more and more deeply in love with Jesus, and here was this elderly woman telling me that my enthusiasm and my delight were just a phase I was going through and that it would soon pass! I can remember standing in the foyer of the church as she walked off and praying in my head, "Lord, do not let me become like that old woman. Please don't let me settle!"

The second incident took place exactly one week after the one I have just recounted. Once again, it took place after the Sunday evening service in the church building. This time an elderly man approached me. The first part of the conversation was almost exactly the same as the one I had had with the old lady the week before. It was what the old man said at the end of the conversation that was so different. Instead of him telling me that my passion and energy was just a phase, this old man looked at me and said, "Son, keep going! I've been a Christian for over sixty years and it gets better and better as the years go by." I can remember thinking that it couldn't possibly get better than it was at that moment, but I can also remember seeing the glint of godliness in that old man's eyes. There was something about him. He shone out the glory of God. His very face had a radiance about it. As he walked away, I can remember asking God to make me like that old man.

Looking back at those two incidents helps me to remember the choice I made then and the choice I continue to make. I don't want to be like the old woman who was cynical and resigned to a faith that was fading out. I want to be like the old man, whose faith was blazing brightly and who was continually growing and being strengthened in his relationship with God.

The danger of nostalgia

Since that time, I have been pastoring churches for many years, and I have met many, many people who look to the past for a moment when God was doing something that they now miss. Sometimes it causes them to look forward with great anticipation, but often it causes them to look back and yearn for the "good old days". It's particularly challenging when you are a new pastor in a church. You can find yourself constantly told about the way things used to be. It can be incredibly discouraging if you are not careful. I don't think anyone who looks back wants it to be discouraging to you as a new pastor, but it can be.

Nostalgia is a wistful desire to return in thought or in fact to a former time in your life, to your home or homeland, or to your family and friends; it is a sentimental yearning for the happiness of a former place or time. There are many people who cannot escape the past because they want to live in it. They remember a moment when God was closer and more real, and they want that moment back. There is nothing wrong with the desire to be intimate with God once again. Indeed, we should all have a yearning to grow in intimacy and in love with God. When we try to recreate the past, however, we are making a mistake. There is an old saying that goes something like this: the past is history, the future is a mystery, but today is a gift – that is why it is called the present. We are not called to live in the past, and we are certainly not called to recreate it. We are not called to live in the future either, although we are called to lay good foundations for it. We are called to live in today, this moment, this generation.

The danger with nostalgia is that it tells us lies. It paints a picture of the past that manages to either edit out the dark colours of our struggles, despairs, and mistakes, or it changes our memory of them so we think we handled them in a better way than we did. Nostalgia draws us backwards and ties us to the events of the past rather than propelling us into the possibilities of today and tomorrow. Nostalgia tries to recreate a moment that is gone by peddling the lie that if we recreate the moment, we will be as happy *now* as we were *then*. I have seen nostalgia at work in a whole variety of situations.

In a church in Devon where I was once interviewed to be the new pastor, one of the elders had seen a remarkable miracle in the late 1940s when a man had been raised from the dead. In my discussions with the church in the 1990s, this elder was still one of the church leaders and he repeatedly asked me if I believed that God could still raise people from the dead. Each time, I answered with a very definite "yes". It became clear as my interview progressed that this elder was living for a moment that had taken place fifty years before. He couldn't move on because he was caught up with the glory of the moment he had experienced fifty years earlier. I didn't accept the call to pastor that church because I felt that the church was trying to travel backwards and not forwards.

I pastored a church in Bournemouth for seven years and loved every minute of it. The elders became dear friends, and together we would rejoice in what the Lord was doing and seek to lay good foundations for what would come after us. There was a particular person in the church family, however, who had sat on the knee of George Jeffreys, the founder of the Elim Pentecostal Church. Each time I went to speak to her she would tell me that she wished she had been able to stay in the Royal Albert Hall on Easter Monday in the years when George Jeffreys would baptize thousands of people. Of course, I understood that she was really yearning for the power and the presence of the Lord again, but she was longing to go backwards instead of forwards. Her memory was more powerful than her yearning.

I've seen nostalgia destroy marriages because a husband or a wife wanted to recreate a moment in their past. I've seen nostalgia undermine new ventures because people weren't able to think of a different future. They'd rather see a business close or a ministry die than try something new. I've seen nostalgia change facts about a whole nation's past, whether that be Christians repainting the past in the UK with much more gospel colour than was actually present, or Americans looking back and omitting the dark chapters of their history because they were too difficult to look at.

Nostalgia manifests itself in many ways, but its results are always the same. We can feel better about ourselves by looking backwards to a time when we were happier, or to a place where we were more content. The greatest danger of being driven by nostalgia is that it can lead us to attempt to recreate the past. In doing that, we miss the fact that God is a God of the living. He is the God who speaks today and brings hope today. Nostalgia and hope cannot both flourish in our lives at the same time.

Honouring the past and building for the future

So am I suggesting that we should not think about the past and that we should simply focus our attention on the here and now? I am not saying that at all. I am suggesting that it is possible to have a better approach to the past. We can remember it with thanksgiving, we can learn from it in humility, and we can celebrate the good things about it, but at the same time we should look around at the here and the now and see what God is doing today, and we can build for the future.

The people of Israel were masters at telling the stories of their past. They used these stories as launch pads for trust in the here and now, though. The Bible is full of examples of the positive and powerful use of memory. The refrain, "Give thanks to the LORD, for he is good; for his steadfast love endures forever" is a constant cry of the saints (Psalm 107:1; 118:1, 29; 136:1; 1 Chronicles 16:34). Looking backwards to remember the goodness of God is a powerful tool for us in our continuing journey with God. What we must not do is try to stay in the past.

Not only that, but the leaders of Israel used the past as a means of creating yearning for a different future. In the period of the Restoration in Israel, when the Temple was being rebuilt, Haggai used the memory of the old Temple as a means of encouragement for the Jews to take up the work of rebuilding the Temple:

> Who is left among you that saw this house in its former glory? How does it look to you now? Is it not in your sight as nothing? Yet now take courage, O Zerubbabel, says the LORD; take courage, O Joshua, son of Jehozadak, the high priest; take courage, all you people of the land, says the LORD; work, for I am with you, says the LORD of hosts, according to the promise that I made you when you came out of Egypt. My spirit abides among you; do not fear … The latter splendor of this house shall be greater than the former, says the LORD of hosts; and in this place I will give prosperity, says the LORD of hosts.
>
> **Haggai 2:3-5, 9**

We see the same sentiment used by Ezra, Nehemiah, Malachi, and Zechariah as they ministered into the midst of a community that was returning from Babylon to Jerusalem and seeking to rebuild the Temple and the city. Memory can spur us on to good things. It can propel us into a bright and new future. To do so, however, we must be careful not to be fixated on the past.

Radicals, progressives, conservatives, traditionalists

I believe every church has four groups of people in it. They are the radicals, the progressives, the conservatives, and the traditionalists. If I were to portray them in a continuum, it would look something like this:

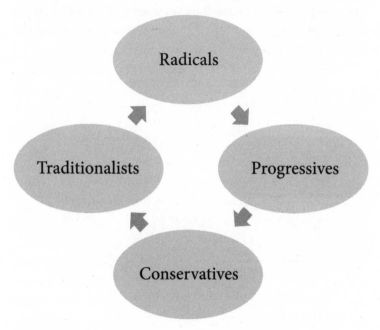

Which one describes you? I admit my descriptions are a little tongue in cheek, but you will catch what I am trying to say.

The radicals are the ones who want everything to change, and they want it to change now. They are not good at celebrating the past and they see little in it to be thankful for. They don't like focusing on what was at all.

They want to move forward, break new ground, and try new things. They think the organ is a demonic creation and that it should be ripped out and burned! They want everything to change, and they are impatient with anyone who gets in the way. They understand the progressives but think they are just not determined enough. They really don't understand the thinking of the conservatives and the traditionalists. What they don't realize is that they are actually quite like the traditionalists in temperament and outlook; they are just looking in a different direction.

The progressives want to move things forward. They are restless with the status quo. They think there are some things in the past that are good, although not many! They want the organ to stay but not really to be played, except at weddings and funerals. They want to get as many people on board as possible, but they are willing to take risks and move things along. They want to go a little slower than the radicals but they have great sympathy with the radical view, although they also have sympathy for and understand the conservatives. They don't get the traditionalists, though!

The conservatives think that we have a duty to defend the past. They understand the need for change, but they don't want too much to change. They acknowledge that we should move with the times, but they are also rather suspicious of the times! They are willing to embark on change, but not anything too significant or too important. The organ should stay. It should be played regularly, and we should sing more hymns! They understand the progressives' desire for change and they have great sympathy with the traditionalists' desire to guard their heritage, but they don't get the radicals, who just seem to dislike everything.

The traditionalists don't think anything needs to change. They see themselves as the guardians of the heritage of the church. They will fight tooth and nail any suggestion that change needs to happen. They think drums are demonic and that the organ should be the only instrument played in church! They don't like all this modern rubbish creeping into the church, like projectors and café-style services and the internet and small groups! They appreciate the conservatives' view of things but they have no time for the progressives, and they really don't like the radicals. They don't realize that they are quite similar to the radicals, however, because they are facing in the opposite direction.

So which description fits you? I bet you are thinking about other people in your church family and categorizing them too! It can be very enlightening to think about this for a while, and it can also be helpful to think about it as a team, a small group or a church leadership. Understanding what kind of person you are helps you to understand how you react to other people.

Here is an even more interesting question, though: which one of these categories describes Jesus?

I am utterly convinced that Jesus was a radical traditionalist. He told his disciples that not even the smallest part of the law would be obliterated or removed (Matthew 5:18), and you cannot get much more traditional than that. He attended synagogue, prayed regularly, and observed all the requirements of Judaism as set out in the Torah. Yet he was also a radical. He said that he had come to welcome sinners and the sick, not the self-righteous and the apparently perfect (Luke 5:31). When he announced his ministry and its focus in the synagogue in Nazareth (Luke 4), he quoted Isaiah 61, but he challenged those who were defending the traditions of the rabbi to the very core. By embracing the radical and the traditional viewpoint, Jesus encompassed the progressive and the conservative worldview too.

There is a great lesson here for us – a lesson that we also see in the attitude of the apostle Paul.

Lessons from Philippians 3

Paul writes to the Christians in Philippi, encouraging them to stay focused on what God has for them. He wants their full gaze and attention to be given to what God has for them as they progress in their faith in Christ. Paul tells them that they should be careful not to be dragged backwards to practices, habits, and worldviews that will not help them now (Philippians 3:1–2). He then goes on to say that his view of what is important and central in his life has been radically changed by his encounter with Christ (Philippians 3:3–7). Paul's central focus has become what Christ has achieved for him. Nothing else is nearly as important to Paul as the aim of becoming all that Christ has called him to be (Philippians 3:8–11). As Paul draws his arguments to a close, he tells the Philippians that he has not finished the journey. There is more for Paul to understand in Christ. There is more for Paul to experience in Christ. Absolutely nothing is as important as pressing in to what God has for Paul in Christ:

> Not that I have already obtained this or have
> already reached the goal; but I press on to make
> it my own, because Christ Jesus has made me his
> own. Beloved, I do not consider that I have made

> it my own; but this one thing I do: forgetting what
> lies behind and straining forward to what lies
> ahead, I press on toward the goal for the prize of
> the heavenly call of God in Christ Jesus.

Philippians 3:12–14

These same principles can help us not to become people who try to recreate the past or who become wedged in what used to be.

- We must not allow old practices and habits to be more important than our new identity in Christ.

- We must allow Christ to be central in our lives. He is not someone who stands on the edge of our circles; he is the centre of our circles. Our lives now revolve around him.

- There is more for us to learn about who we are in Christ, and this is now the priority of our lives. All other competing influences are secondary.

- As long as we are alive, Christ is shaping and forming us, and we are being made more and more like him.

In Robert Browning's poem, "Rabbi Ben Ezra", we read the words:

> Grow old along with me!
> The best is yet to be,
> The last of life, for which the first was made:
> Our times are in His hand.

Robert Browning, "Rabbi Ben Ezra"

There is a sense in which that captures the essence of what I am trying to say – the best is yet to be. Do not let the distorted memory of a glorious past rob you of the glorious promise of a transformed tomorrow.

So many people look back to a point in the history of their lives and long for it to be recreated. If only they could have stayed there, they think. Yet there is something deeply, deeply wrong about such a sentiment. Christian hope doesn't drag you back; it moves you forward. The best days of the Christian's life are not the days that once were; they are the days that are yet to be. Individually and collectively, God's people are continually being changed from one degree of glory to another (2 Corinthians 3:18). The church's best days are not the days that lie in the past; they are the days that lie ahead of us. God will build his church (Matthew 16:18), and God will build each one of us (Philippians 1:6). He will take us through every trial and storm and difficulty and hardship, and through them he will fashion greater and greater Christlikeness in us (James 1:3–4). It is not sentimental gibberish for Christians to declare that the end of our lives is greater than the beginning; it is good theology. It is the fundamental basis of Christian hope. The best is yet to be. If you believe it, then lift up your head and let it shape your decisions about today and tomorrow.

God gazers look backwards with thanks and with honesty, but they look forward with anticipation and hope. We know that our futures are stronger than our pasts. We know that the God who drew us to himself is also drawing us forward. We have felt the hand of the Spirit upon our lives, drawing us into new discoveries of grace. We are not content to stay locked in a past world; we want to see a new kingdom grow. We are drawn forward by the mercy and grace and goodness of God. We know that there are glorious things in our past, but we know that there are mistakes and failings there too. Yet we know that our adventure of faith will take us to new places and will change us even more deeply. Like Abraham, Isaac, and Jacob, we have learned that we are called to be pilgrims and travellers in this life (1 Peter 2:11–12).

The book of Exodus is the story of a people who have left Egypt and the oppression of a foreign king and are walking to freedom in Canaan. To be a Christian is to have left the Egypt of our old lives and to have entered the Canaan of victorious Christian living. We are being drawn towards all that God has for us. It is a fundamental act of faith to believe that God has not finished with us yet.

If we have failed, we can start again. Nothing in our past compares to the glorious future that lies ahead of us. Nelson Mandela, in his remarkable autobiography, said:

> I am fundamentally an optimist. Whether that comes from nature or nurture, I cannot say. Part of being optimistic is keeping one's head pointed toward the sun, one's feet moving forward. There were many dark moments when my faith in humanity was sorely tested, but I would not and could not give myself up to despair. That way lays defeat and death.[4]

God gazers are not just optimists; we are also people of faith. God gazers are nurtured by the presence and the power of the Holy Spirit. We are given the nature of Christ.

---

4 Nelson Rolihlahla Mandela, *Long Walk to Freedom: The Autobiography of Nelson Mandela*, London: Little, Brown and Company, 1995, p.391.

God is at work in us. We do not point our head toward the sun; we fix our gaze upon the Son. There are many dark moments in our lives, and there are many moments when our faith is sorely tested, but we refuse to give ourselves up to despair. We know that going backwards is not an option. We are too busy for the kingdom and all that lies ahead to be drawn back to yesterday. We are not living for the halcyon days of a bygone era; we are fixed on the hopeful future that God has for us.

CHAPTER FIVE

Beyond the Trappings of Success

I want to be a God gazer!
Looking beyond the trappings of success,
cutting through the stucco of respectability
like a laser piercing darkness.

"What will it profit them to gain the whole world
and forfeit their life?"

Mark 8:36

oney really doesn't buy happiness.

Having money is not a token of success.

You can appear wealthy and successful and still be miserable.

Ask Georgia and Patterson Inman. Their story was told in *Rolling Stone* magazine in August 2013. They are heirs to the Duke family fortune, set to inherit well over one billion dollars. Their family made their money in tobacco. Yet Georgia and Patterson suffered the most horrendous upbringing and have spent a great deal of time in therapy.

Ask Christina Crawford. Her mother was Joan Crawford, the famous Hollywood actress. Despite living a life of luxury, Christina told the story of misery and neglect in her autobiography, *Mommie Dearest*.

The litany of lives that have had wealth and power and prestige yet not discovered happiness goes on and on and on. Robin Williams, Peaches Geldof, Casey Johnson, Amy Winehouse, Michael Jackson, Whitney Houston… Talented, gifted, entertaining, and loved people whose lives crashed and burned despite their wealth and popularity. Their stories make the headlines, but many other people's don't.

The simple and fundamental reality is that money doesn't make you happy. Benjamin Franklin once said that money had never made people happy and nor would it ever be able to do so. He argued that there was nothing in its nature that could produce happiness, but that it was addictive. Unless you have a stronger power in your life, the reality is that the more money you have, the more you want.

The power of money is exerted not only over those who are obsessed with having more and more of it. The power of money is also seen in the lives of those who have known what it is to be poor and then become petrified of poverty. Cher once said that she was scared to death of being poor. She likened it to an overweight girl who loses 500 pounds but always feels fat on the inside. Cher said she grew up poor and always felt poor inside. She described is as her "paranoia".

We live in an age where money and success have almost become synonymous. Yet there are many successful people who have little to no money. My mother has lived a successful life. She brought up five children. She has never been wealthy and her success cannot be measured in the number of books she has sold or how well known she is, but her life has been one that has been invested in others. Gandhi was not wealthy, neither was Martin Luther King, but their lives left a legacy. Pope John Paul II was not wealthy; Pope Benedict XVI and Pope Francis are not wealthy men, but their lives have been successful.

The measure of success

What makes a person successful? If it isn't the wealth that they accumulate and the possessions that they gather around them, what is it? The story is told of a man who died and his friends and family began discussing his life after the funeral. The discussion drifted to what assets he had left behind, and someone asked, "What did he leave?" The answer was given simply by one of his family members: "He left everything. Don't we all?"

To many people today, the notion of success is inseparable from wealth, possessions, and power. The pinnacle of achievement is to have your name appear in *The Sunday Times* Rich List, or *Forbes*. Success and influence is measured in dollars or airtime. Where I live, a great deal of effort and time is put into making sure you are in the country set. Mixing with the right people, driving the right car, having your children attend the right schools, having the best address, marrying into the right family, studying at the right university: these all become badges of honour and success and measures of worth and value. Yet they are such transitory things. They are certainly not what the Bible uses as a measure for success, and they are not high on the list of Jesus' criteria for success.

Jesus tells the story of a man who was increasingly successful but extremely foolish:

> And he said to them, "Take care! Be on your guard
> against all kinds of greed; for one's life does not
> consist in the abundance of possessions." Then
> he told them a parable: "The land of a rich man
> produced abundantly. And he thought to himself,
> 'What should I do, for I have no place to store
> my crops?' Then he said, 'I will do this: I will pull
> down my barns and build larger ones, and there I
> will store all my grain and my goods. And I will say
> to my soul, Soul, you have ample goods laid up for
> many years; relax, eat, drink, be merry.' But God
> said to him, 'You fool! This very night your life is
> being demanded of you. And the things you have
> prepared, whose will they be?' So it is with those
> who store up treasures for themselves but are not
> rich toward God."
>
> **Luke 12:15–21**

The implications are clear. Material possessions and wealth are not the measure of our success. But money and possessions are not inherently wrong, either. It is not money that is the root of all evil; it is the love of money or the obsession with money that is the root of all kinds of evil (1 Timothy 6:10). We can do a great deal of good with money and with possessions. The issue is not whether we have these things or not; the issue is whether these things have us.

The key to understanding biblical success lies in understanding that whatever has our heart also has our lives. As Jesus goes on to say in the passage above, where our treasure is demonstrates where our heart lies (Matthew 6:21; Luke 12:33–34).

Christian faith defines success according to whether our lives are bringing glory to God. We are successful when we pursue God's purposes for the world and his call upon our lives. For some, this might mean that we end up in places of wealth and privilege and influence, but these attainments will not shape us. The Christian does not let their wealth or their possessions or their position determine their value and their dignity. For the follower of Christ, doing the will of God in faithfulness is the measure of success. Popularity, power, position, and prowess are nothing but shadows that come and go. Jesus experienced this himself. The same people who cried out, "Hosanna to the son of David," and welcomed him to Jerusalem were crying out, "Crucify him!" just a week later (John 19:15). In fact, Jesus' own life is a wonderful example of what success really looks like.

Jesus was never a man of material wealth and power. Paul makes it clear that Jesus, although he was rich, for our sakes became poor so that we through his poverty might be made rich. The argument Paul is making is directly connected to Jesus' material and positional wealth that were given up to make us spiritually rich (2 Corinthians 8:9). Jesus never wrote a book, yet he has influenced more people than anyone else in the history of the world. He never travelled beyond a small area of land in the Middle East, yet his teaching has transformed governments, societies, and individuals. He was never the commander of a vast army, yet his life has shaped more people than any general or commander or emperor.

He was never a political leader. He never married. He never owned a house. He did not come to establish a religion and he was not a philosopher or an engineer. At the end of his earthy life he was murdered as a political dissident on trumped-up charges on a hill just outside a second-rate provincial town, and no one in the wider Roman world took much interest. Yet his life is the most gloriously successful, the most wonderfully *alive life* that has ever been witnessed.

The life of Jesus shows us that a successful life is not measured by bank balances or by what we own. Instead it is measured by whether or not we have lived according to God's plans and purposes, and whether we have fulfilled his calling in our lives.

A life lived on purpose

Jesus himself made it clear what it means to live well. He said that the secret to a successful life is to love God with all our heart, soul, mind, and strength and to love our neighbours as we love ourselves (Matthew 22:37–40). In the end, this is the fundamental reality that we must face. Did I love God? Did I love others? Did I love the person God made me to be? Was I true to what God wanted me to be? There can be no more penetrating question.

As a pastor, I have the privilege of walking the road towards death and heaven with many people. Often, as someone approaches the end their life, I will talk with them about their regrets and the things that they want to deal with. It is an important part of pastoral ministry to help people die well. In the years that I have been pastoring I have stood besides hundreds of people on their deathbed. I have never heard anyone tell me that they wished they had spent more time at the office. I have never heard anyone tell me that they wished they had made more money. I have never had anyone tell me that they regretted failing an exam. I have had some people tell me that they wished they had given more time to their families. I have had some people tell me they wished they had given God more time and space. I have had some tell me they wished they had been more gracious or generous or gentle. I have had many tell me they wished that they had been more open with the people they loved and were preparing to leave. It is in the last moments of our lives that we demonstrate what is the most important part of our living.

Harry and Sally Henderson were very special people to me. Sally was from Wales and Harry was from my homeland, Northern Ireland. They were a couple who loved Jesus deeply, and loved one another deeply. They loved their four children, their grandchildren, and their great-grandchildren deeply too. Sally died in May 2014 and her husband, Harry, died in August of the same year. Their deaths were separated by just fifteen weeks. They lived successful lives! Like all of us, they made mistakes, I am sure. Harry and Sally Henderson lived with God at the centre of their lives, though. Serving Christ in the UK and in various other countries around the world, they gave the best of their lives to God, to one another, and to their children and their family. They left a mark. Their lives mattered. They were not impressed with whether people were wealthy or powerful or popular. Harry and Sally cared about one thing, and one thing only, and that was living the lives that God wanted them to live. They did this beautifully, and I miss them very much.

Sally wanted a poem read at her service of thanksgiving, called "The Guy in the Glass". Peter Dale Wimbrow Sr wrote the poem in the 1930s, but Sally had read it in a daily devotional called *Word for Today*.

> When you get what you want in your struggle
> for pelf,
> And the world makes you King for a day,
> Then go to the mirror and look at yourself,
> And see what that guy has to say.
>
> For it isn't your Father, or Mother, or Wife,
> Who judgment upon you must pass.
> The feller whose verdict counts most in your life
> Is the guy staring back from the glass.
>
> He's the feller to please, never mind all the rest,
> For he's with you clear up to the end
> And you've passed your most dangerous,
> difficult test
> If the guy in the glass is your friend.
>
> …
>
> You can fool the whole world down the pathway
> of years,
> And get pats on the back as you pass,
> But your final reward will be heartache and tears
> If you've cheated the guy in the glass.

Peter Dale Wimbrow, Sr, "The Guy in the Glass"[5]

God gazers know that the greatest measure of success is <u>whether or not</u> they have been true to the person God has

5   The full poem can be found at http://www.theguyintheglass.com/gig.htm

made them to be. They recognize that at the end of their lives, they will stand before another and give an account of how they have lived. They want to be able to say that they lived and died well. God gazers know that they find themselves most fully alive when they are alive in Christ. They understand that their purpose and meaning and significance flow from the fact that they are made in the image of God and that they have been redeemed by the grace of God. God gazers will not define themselves by what other people think of them. They will be true to God and to what God has called them to be.

If you are a pastor or a church leader and a God gazer, then don't let yourself be defined by the number of people who come to the church you lead or by the size of your building or by the amount of money in your offerings. Allow yourself to be defined by God's love for you, his purpose for your life, and his grace manifested in you. Twenty years from now few people will remember the specific sermon you preached on a given Sunday, but many will remember what you said at their loved one's funeral. Few, if any, will be able to talk about the great series you preached in such and such a year, but they will remember whether you were kind and whether you remembered their name and showed them the love of God.

If you are a mother or a father and a God gazer, your children will not remember what gift you gave them on what birthday. They will remember whether you told them you loved them. They will remember your approval, your acceptance, and your love. They will remember the fact that you told them the truth even when it hurt.

If you are a son or a daughter and a God gazer, there will come a day when you will look back on your life and either thank God that you honoured your parents and you did all you could to love them and support them, or regret not having done so.

I could go on and on, but you do not need me to.

Don't let yourself be defined by the wrong criteria. Don't fall into the trap of assessing yourself in the light of what culture describes as successful. Instead, allow the biblical definition of success to define you. Act justly, love mercy, and walk humbly before your God (Micah 6:8).

One last thing. Don't beat yourself up over this. If you, like me, have made mistakes in how you understand success, then breathe out. You have time to change your priorities. Take a few moments to look into the heart of God now. He is right there beside you, and he is far more willing to give you another chance than you are to take it. The mistakes of the past do not have to define the decisions of the future. Don't define yourself the wrong way, and don't define the people around you the wrong way either. Whatever your mistakes might have been, they can be opportunities to try a new approach and to have a fresh start.

God loves you. God has a wonderful purpose for you. God crafted you to make a difference in the world. Just be faithful to what he has called you to be.

CHAPTER SIX

Becoming Fluent

I want to be a God gazer!
Reaching for the stars and
seeing beauty in the moment by
becoming fluent in the language
of the God who is here, who is now.

Wait for the LORD;
be strong and take heart
and wait for the LORD.

Psalm 27:14 (NIV)

There is no place on this planet where God is not. That means that whatever you are facing, whatever you are going through, God is present in it with you. He is not distant, watching with ambivalence. He is present, longing to help and support and carry you. He is not far away, squinting at you through the mists of culture or time. He is present, able to understand and help and support you in the very context of here and now. You do not have to look very far to see God. You can see him in the very breath that you exhale on a winter morning, if you are willing to look hard enough. You can see him in the face of the person you will sit beside on the train today, if you will only take the time to look. Our problem is not that God is hiding from us. Our problem is that we are too busy, or too preoccupied, or too fast, to see him.

The God who is here

Francis Schaeffer's book *The God Who is There* is a powerful call for Christians to engage with the world around us and be faithful to the gospel of Jesus Christ as given to us in the Bible. It is an important book for the church today because it reminds us that we are guardians and stewards of the gospel, but that the gospel does not belong to us. If Schaeffer's call is to recognize that God is in the church and in the world, that God is *there* wherever *there* might be, then I want to take his illustration and drive it even closer to home, because the God who is there is also the God who is here.

God is right where you are at this very moment. He is not some distant construct of a deist's mind, detached from the world and uninterested in what happens on the earth. He is present. Present in the struggles and the challenges of our lives. Present on each continent of the earth. He does not turn his back on us. He doesn't pretend that he is not looking. He does not force us to follow him. But nor does he leave us alone. God has revealed himself to us in Christ. He has given us his name, and it is the name that he invites us to use in personal relationship with himself.

One of the great dichotomies of Christian faith is that God invites us to know him, and it is only as we turn to face him that we grow to know him better. The truth of any relationship is true of a relationship with God. In order to get to know him better we must engage in a relationship with him. It is never enough to know *about* God if we are to deepen our understanding of him. Instead, we must walk with him. We can do this because he has come to us *as one of us*. He has dressed himself in our humanity, experienced our pain, and walked our road. God has taken a human face in Jesus Christ. We can see what he looks like, listen to his words, and follow his footsteps. We are not groping in the dark. He has shown himself to us. We do not need to search the far-flung places of the universe to find God: he has walked upon the earth, left his footprints in the ground, and touched the very fabric of our existence in the life and teaching of Jesus Christ, a carpenter from Nazareth who was also the Son of God. This same God is now present throughout the earth by the power of the Holy Spirit. He is visible through the hands and feet and voice and heart of his body, the church, and he is still committed to revealing himself to those who will look to him.

God gazers are not looking for God somewhere else because they have come to understand that he is right here, right now, and this realization changes their lives. They do not need to ask what he looks like because they have seen him in the face of Jesus. They do not need to ask what he would say because he has spoken through his Son and through the Bible. They do not need to ask where he is because his Holy Spirit is present across the face of the earth. They have come to understand that there is no place where God is not, and this makes all the difference in their lives.

The powerful yet present God

There are two great words used to describe the whereabouts and the magnitude of God that I want to explore with you, and those words are "transcendent" and "immanent". The word "transcendent" means "above everything". Transcendent means all powerful. Transcendent means all present. Transcendent means all knowing. God is all of these things. He is all knowing, he is all present and he is all powerful. These are big ideas. Through the years of the church's history when her theologians wrote in Latin, the prefix *omni* became associated with these ideas because it means "all". God is omnipotent (all powerful), omniscient (all knowing) and omnipresent (all present). Hence we can read the words of the King David:

> Where can I go from your spirit?
> Or where can I flee from your presence?
> If I ascend to heaven, you are there;
> if I make my bed in Sheol, you are there.
> If I take the wings of the morning
> and settle at the farthest limits of the sea,
> even there your hand shall lead me,
> and your right hand shall hold me fast.
> If I say, "Surely the darkness shall cover me,
> and the light around me become night,"
> even the darkness is not dark to you;
> the night is as bright as the day,
> for darkness is as light to you.

King David, Psalm 139:7–12

God, the transcendent God, is everywhere. He sees all things, he knows all things, and he is more powerful than all things.

What, then, of the idea of God's immanence? This word means that God is not only there; he is also here. God is present. God is personal. God is knowable. A God who is transcendent alone would be a frightening prospect. He would be remote and far away. Such a God would be hard to reach and even harder, if not impossible, to relate to. Christianity does not believe that God is *only* transcendent, however. Christianity also teaches that God is present. He is close. He is near.

Karl Barth argued powerfully in his *Church Dogmatics* that God is here, there, and everywhere, and that argument captures the heart of what I am trying to say here. God is not only all powerful, but he is also intimately present with his people and throughout the world. Allow me to illustrate his closeness through the use of three basic ideas in the Bible.

Emmanuel

In the annunciation of the conception of Jesus, Mary was told:

> All this took place to fulfill what had been spoken by the Lord through the prophet:
>
> "Look, the virgin shall conceive and bear a son, and they shall name him Emmanuel," which means, "God is with us".
>
> **Matthew 1:22–23, cf. Isaiah 7:14**

97

The name "Emmanuel", which means "God is with us", only appears three times in the Bible. It can be found in Isaiah 7:14, 8:8 and in Matthew 1:23, but it leads to the most startling declaration imaginable. Jesus, the Son of Mary, was God himself who came to live among people on the earth. You cannot get any nearer than to live among people as one of us. Jesus did not pretend to be human; he was a fully human being. At the heart of Christian faith is the conviction that Jesus was 100% divine and 100% human. In fact, the earliest confessions and creeds of the Christian church declared this to be true:

> I believe in God the Father Almighty, Creator of
> the heavens and the earth.
> I believe in Jesus Christ, his only Son, our Lord,
> Who was conceived by the Holy Spirit and born of
> the Virgin Mary...

The Apostles' Creed [6]

The idea that Jesus Christ is God enrobed in flesh is central to the teaching of the New Testament and fundamental to any biblical understanding of who Jesus is and what he came to do. It is because God has come to us in Christ that we can be sure of what God is like, because Jesus shows us what God is like. Jesus is the "Word become flesh", and he has dwelt among us in such a way that we can see God in him and he clearly shows us what God is like (John 1). Jesus himself said that anyone who had seen him had seen the Father (John 14:9); he made it clear that he had come only to speak what the Father wanted

---

6   Please see my book, *Unbelievable: Confident Faith in a Sceptical World*, for an unpacking of the Apostles' Creed, Oxford, Monarch, 2014.

him to speak (John 12:49) and only to do what the Father wanted him to do (John 14:30–31). Furthermore, we can relate to God through Jesus with confidence precisely because Jesus came as Emmanuel. Jesus has endured the same temptations as we have, but without sin; he has been impacted by the same challenges and decisions as we have, so he understands what we face because he faced it too. He is a perfect representative for us before God because he perfectly represented God to us:

> Since, then, we have a great high priest who has
> passed through the heavens, Jesus, the Son of God,
> let us hold fast to our confession. For we do not
> have a high priest who is unable to sympathize
> with our weaknesses, but we have one who in every
> respect has been tested as we are, yet without sin.
> Let us therefore approach the throne of grace with
> boldness, so that we may receive mercy and find
> grace to help in time of need.
>
> **Hebrews 4:14–16**

The importance of Christ as one of us cannot be overstated. He lived a perfect human life. He endured the punishment for our sins as a human upon the cross. He stands before God now as a perfect human. All of this flows from God's *closeness* to us in Jesus. We do not need to guess what God is like because we see him in the face, life, and actions of Jesus Christ (Colossians 1; 1 John 1).

Yahweh, I am

The second simple illustration of the closeness of God is the central name that God gives himself. I say the central name because there are many other names for God given to us in the Bible. He is our banner, our healer, our shepherd, our provider, our rock, our shoulder, our high tower, and many other things. Central to all of these names, and central to our understanding of God, is the central name that he has given himself, the core way in which he has chosen to reveal himself. The story of the revelation of this name to Moses is told in Exodus 3:

> But Moses said to God, "If I come to the Israelites and say to them, 'The God of your ancestors has sent me to you,' and they ask me, 'What is his name?' what shall I say to them?" God said to Moses, "I AM WHO I AM." He said further, "Thus you shall say to the Israelites, 'I AM has sent me to you.'" God also said to Moses, "Thus you shall say to the Israelites, 'The LORD, the God of your ancestors, the God of Abraham, the God of Isaac, and the God of Jacob, has sent me to you':

> This is my name forever,
> and this my title for all generations."

> **Exodus 3:13–15**

The name translated "I am" in this passage is the word *Yahweh*. It is notoriously difficult to translate into English but it means, "I am as I will always be", or "I am always", or "I am continually being". There are many other variations, but I am sure you understand the sentiment. God reveals himself to Moses as the God who always is. Not only that, but this very idea of God always being is picked up in the New Testament in several ways. Firstly, it is used to illustrate that God does not change: he is utterly reliable and he is the living God. He *is* the God of Abraham and he *is* the God of Isaac and he *is* the God of Jacob. His nature, character, and commitment are unchanging. Secondly, the apostle John picks up the title of "I am" and attributes it to the very words of Jesus himself. In John's Gospel, Jesus repeatedly uses the phrase "I am" to describe himself. Indeed, the whole of the narrative and structure of John's Gospel is built around these famous "I am" sayings:

- I am the bread of life (John 6:35,48)
- I am the light of the world (John 8:12; 9:5)
- Before Abraham was, I am (John 8:58)
- I am the gate (John 10:9)
- I am the good shepherd (John 10:11)
- I am the resurrection and the life (John 11:25)
- I am the way, the truth, and the life (John 14:6)
- I am the true vine (John 15:1)

God is not distant; he is close. He is the present and living "I am". The God who has come to us in Christ is the same God who upholds the world. He is the same God who conversed with Abraham, Isaac, Jacob, Moses, and David. He is the God who comes to us, because we could never reach him on our own. He is the God who comes to us and reveals himself to us (Romans 5) and then invites a response from us. He is the God who loved us before we ever loved him (1 John 4:19).

I will never leave you

My third simple word picture is found in the phrase, "I will never leave you nor fail or forsake you." This promise was given to Moses (Deuteronomy 31:6), to Joshua (Joshua 1:5, 9), and then to the Christians who received the letter to the Hebrews (Hebrews 13:5–6), and through that promise it also applies to all who trust in Christ. It is in this promise that we see the most remarkable closeness of God. He is with his people everywhere. He cares enough to be close to us (Proverbs 18:24; Hebrews 13:5); he is with us in the trials and tribulations of our lives and working out his purposes (Romans 8:28); we can throw our cares upon him because we know he cares for us (Psalm 55:22; 1 Peter 5:7); he has promised to be with us until the end of time and to the end of the world (Matthew 28:20; Acts 1:4–8); and he is the God who is present with his church always (Revelation 1–3).

This assurance of his presence in all and in every situation is what makes the great difference in our lives. God is not distant; he is close. Were he present without being all powerful, however, his presence would make little difference to us. Yet we know that he is present *and* powerful. He is *transcendent* and *immanent*. It is this remarkable combination that fills God's people with hope and changes the way we view our situations because, no matter how difficult or dark our lives might feel, God is present with us.

You are not alone. God, who is Emmanuel, is with you.

You are not alone. God, who always is and is always, is with you.

You are not alone. God, who has promised to be with you, keeps his promises.

What does this mean?

To become fluent in the language of the God who is here and who is now means that we learn to see him in the very situations where we are most fearful that he has gone. We learn to see him with us as we rise and as we rest. We remember that there is no situation that we face alone. We remind ourselves that even if we do not see him, feel him, or hear him, he is here.

To become fluent in the language of the God who is here and who is now means that we listen for the voice of God in the voices of those around us. We look for the evidences of his presence and his leading in the ordinary and everyday things of our lives.

To become fluent in the language of the God who is here and who is now means that we become better at welcoming his presence. We catch a sense of him near us in every aspect of our lives. I do not need to go to the other side of the world to meet with God because he has come from the other side of eternity to meet me. I need never fear whether God will be with me because he is always with me. I need not wonder whether he has abandoned me because he never will.

There are good implications and challenging implications of this truth. When I choose to ignore him and do my own thing, he is still there. I cannot pretend that he is not present. This is a challenging thing. He watches every move I make. He is present, listening to every word I speak. He knows every thought. He understands the intention of my heart. I cannot pull the wool over his eyes. I cannot pretend before him. This makes me vulnerable, but it also gives me permission to be honest because the God who is here and who is now is not some kind of capricious, hateful God who scowls at me and grimaces. He loves me. He has accepted me. He has declared me righteous. He has given me the righteous standing of his Son. This is liberating and freeing and enables me to live differently, to live hopefully. I no longer strive for his approval or his presence; instead I live from the reality that I have his approval and I carry his presence. There is nowhere I can go where God is not.

Knowing that God is with me now means that I can be the person he made me to be. I can reach for the stars without fear of his rejection. I do not need to settle for second best. I am free to live for him, free to live in him, and free to serve him. I can stand before kings and politicians with the authority of God because he stands with me. I can sit with the poor, the broken, and the vulnerable in his strength because he sits with me. I can comfort those who mourn with his comfort. I can preach his word in his power. I can speak over the sick, the bruised, and the hurting with his authority. I can enter the throne room of grace and pray with humility but with confidence because he is with me. I can stand before God because Jesus, my Saviour and my friend, has given me his grace and poured out his Spirit upon me. I can walk through the darkest valley, even death itself, knowing that the shadow is an indication that his light is with me and I am not alone.

I can never be alone.

God gazers are able to face their circumstances with confidence because they know that God is with them. They are able to step into perilous and unknown situations because they know that God goes with them. They sleep knowing God is there. They have a deep assurance in their hearts that God is for them and not against them. God gazers see God in other people. They are able to affirm others without being anxious or being diminished. God gazers see the best in others and believe the best in others because they know that God has placed his Spirit in their hearts. God gazers are fluent in the language of the God who is here and who is now. They know that even in the deepest and darkest night, the light of God still shines. They know that the unexpected and the tragic are not unknown to God. They can face a furnace with the assurance that God is with them, and they can enter a lion's den unafraid because God is with them. They have learned the truth that Christian victory is not the absence of pain, but the presence of Christ.

Are you a God gazer? Have you discovered that whether you live or die, you are his? Do you know the absolute freedom that comes from the rock solid assurance that God is there, God is here, and God is everywhere? Do you have the hope that nothing, absolutely nothing, will ever pluck you from the presence of God?

It is the most remarkable thing to know that, whatever happens, there is one thing that will never happen. The world may end. Our loved ones may be taken from us. We may face illness, torture, and struggle. We may lose everything. We may suffer for Christ. All these things may happen, but God will never, never, never, never leave us.

Of this we can be sure.

CHAPTER SEVEN

Until My Thirst is Sated

I want to be a God gazer!
Until my imagination is saturated;
until my thirst is sated;
until my passion is stirred;
until my intellect is stretched
as far as it can be;
until my yearning yearns
for others to be free.

Ho, everyone who thirsts,
come to the waters;
and you that have no money,
come, buy and eat!
Come, buy wine and milk
without money and without price.

Isaiah 55:1

What does it mean to have an encounter with God? What changes in our lives as a result of such an encounter? Isaiah's powerful encounter with God in Isaiah 6, which inspired the poem that inspired this book, changed everything in the prophet's life. As a result of his encounter, Isaiah had a fresh sense of the greatness of God, a fresh sense of the closeness of God, and a fresh sense of the purposes of God for Isaiah's own life and ministry.

Is it still possible to have such an encounter today? Does God still want to meet with individuals in ways that will change their whole life? It is not only possible; it is also absolutely vital to a genuine Christian faith that we move from the realms of intellectual assent to personal encounter.

The challenge of both the Old and the New Testament narratives is the number of times that individuals had a personal and direct encounter with God. From the very beginning of the story of God's purposes in the world, as told through the creation narratives and the first eleven chapters of the book of Genesis, all the way to the end of the story in a recreated world as described in the book of Revelation, individual people have direct and personal encounters with God's power and purpose and beauty. Adam and Eve spoke with and encountered God directly (Genesis 3), as did Abraham (Genesis 12), Isaac (Genesis 26), Jacob (Genesis 32), and Joseph (Genesis 37, 39–40). The same is true for each of the great characters in the Old Testament, from Moses (Exodus 3) all the way through to the last historical book of Nehemiah and the last prophetic book of Malachi. God met with people.

In the New Testament he continued to do the same, from the Virgin Mary the mother of Jesus to Joseph, who was Jesus' earthly father (Matthew 1), to Elizabeth and Zechariah, Jesus' aunt and uncle (Luke 1) and John the Baptist, Jesus' cousin (John 1, 3). Every single book of the New Testament is written or dictated by someone who had a direct and personal encounter with the Lord Jesus Christ. The very last book in the Bible, the book of Revelation, is the direct account of a series of personal visions and revelations of Jesus, given to John the disciple by Jesus himself.

The personal encounters with God did not stop with the close of the New Testament. Early church fathers and mothers also wrote and taught about their personal encounters with God. These include people such as Irenaeus of Lyon, who was born in Smyrna in 130 and died in Lugdunum in France in 202; Origen of Alexandria, who was born in Alexandria in 185 and died in Tyre in 254; Tertullian who was born in Carthage in 160 and died in 220; Eusebius who was born in Palestine in 263 and died in 339; Syncletica of Alexandria who was born around 170 and died around 350; Mary of Egypt who was born around 344 and died around 421; Augustine of Hippo who was born in Tagaste in 354 and died in Hippo Regius (Algeria) in 430; and Sarah of the desert who lived and died in the fifth century. Men and women across centuries and across vastly different cultures, social backgrounds, and physical circumstances encountered the power and presence of God.

Augustine of Hippo speaks powerfully of his personal encounter with God in his *Confessions*. As you read his story, particularly books three, five and eight, you hear the confessions of a man who was desperately seeking love and acceptance and meaning. A few excerpts will give you a flavour of his story. They paint a picture of a man desperate for an encounter with God, and the results of that encounter:[7]

---

7 These are my own translations.

I came to Carthage, where a cauldron of unholy loves was seething and bubbling all around me. I was not in love as yet, but I was in love with love; and from a hidden hunger, I hated myself for not feeling more intensely a sense of hunger. I was looking for something to love, for I was in love with loving, and I hated security and a smooth way, free from snares. Within me I had a dearth of that inner food which is thyself, my God – although that dearth caused me no hunger. And I remained without any appetite for incorruptible food – not because I was already filled with it, but because the emptier I became the more I loathed it.

Augustine, *Confessions*, Book Three, Chapter 1

I studied the books of eloquence, for it was in eloquence that I was eager to be eminent, though from a reprehensible and vainglorious motive, and a delight in human vanity. In the ordinary course of study I came upon a certain book of Cicero's… called "Hortensius". Now it was this book which quite definitely changed my whole attitude and turned my prayers towards thee, O Lord and gave me new hope and new desires.

Augustine, *Confessions*, Book Three, Chapter 4

And to Milan I came, to Ambrose the bishop… thy devoted servant. His eloquent discourse in those times abundantly provided thy people with the flour of thy wheat, the gladness of thy oil, and the sober intoxication of thy wine. To him was I led by thee without my knowledge, that by him I might be led to thee in full knowledge…

Augustine, *Confessions*, Book Five ,Chapter 13

Now when deep reflection had drawn up out of the secret depths of my soul all my misery had heaped it up before the sight of my heart, there arose a mighty storm, accompanied by a mighty rain of tears. That I might give way fully to my tears and lamentations, I stole away… for it seemed to me that solitude was more appropriate for the business of weeping… I flung myself under a fig tree – how I know not – and gave free course to my tears. The streams of my eyes gushed out an acceptable sacrifice to thee. And not indeed in these words, but to this effect, I cried to thee: "And thou, O Lord, how long? How long, O Lord? Wilt thou be angry forever? Oh, remember not against us our former iniquities."

I was saying these things… when suddenly I heard the voice of a boy or a girl I know not which – coming from the neighbouring house, chanting over and over and over again, "Pick it up, read it; pick it up, read it." … So, damning the torrent of my tears, I got to my feet, for I could not but think that this was a divine command to open the Bible and read the first passage I should light upon… So I quickly returned to the bench for there I had put down the apostle's book when I left there. I snatched it up, opened it, and in silence read the paragraph on which my eyes first fell: "Not in rioting and drunkenness, not in chambering and wantonness, not in strife and envying, but put on the Lord Jesus Christ, and make no provision for the flesh to fulfill the lusts thereof." I wanted to read no further, nor did I need to. For instantly, as the sentence ended, there was infused in my heart something like the light of full certainty and all the gloom of doubt vanished away.

Augustine, *Confessions*, Book Eight, Chapter 12

What was true for Augustine has been true for millions and millions of Christians down through the years. A tangible and personal encounter with the living God has changed them forever. John Wesley, the great eighteenth-century revivalist preacher and founder of Methodism, had been a clergyman for many years when he finally had a personal encounter with God. Having returned from a visit to America, Wesley had been impacted by a group of Moravian Christians. He attended a meeting in London in May 1738, and he wrote this in his journal on 24 May:

In the evening I went very unwillingly to a society in Aldersgate Street, where one was reading Luther's preface to the Epistle to the Romans. About a quarter before nine, while he was describing the change which God works in the heart through faith in Christ, I felt my heart strangely warmed. I felt I did trust in Christ, Christ alone, for salvation; and an assurance was given me that He had taken away my sins, even mine and saved me from the law of sin and death.

John Wesley, *The Journal of John Wesley*[8]

8   Percy Livingstone Parker (ed.), *The Journal of John Wesley*, Chicago, Moody Press, 1951, entry for 24 May 1738.

My own experience of God's grace is one in which God has spoken clearly to me about his love and compassion for my life. I believe I have heard the audible voice of God twice: once in my conversion in 1986, when I heard the words, "Son, come home," and once in early 1996 when one of my sons was desperately ill and I heard a voice distinctively and clearly tell me, "He's mine." The voice was exactly the same in both cases. Although separated by almost a decade in time, both events had a deep impact upon me. The first led to my conversion and the second led to a deep and settled peace in my heart about my son, Benjamin, despite the uncertainty that he has faced through his life.

Countless people have had direct and personal encounters with God. God has spoken in comfort to those who needed comfort. He has given strength to those who have felt weak. He has given assurance to those who were fearful. In fact, just a few days before the moment that I am writing these words, a friend of mine shared with me how God had met him and his wife while they were on sabbatical and had inspired, invigorated, and renewed them. At Gold Hill just four days ago we welcomed a worship group from the United States called "United Pursuit", and I witnessed God meeting with hundreds and hundreds of people around me as he renewed them, strengthened them, and encouraged them.

God still meets with his people. He still satisfies our thirst. He still refreshes the hearts of the saints. He is able to meet with you today, right where you are. In fact, as Paul told the Christians in Ephesus, God is able to do far more than we could ever dream of:

Now to him who by the power at work within us is able to accomplish abundantly far more than all we can ask or imagine, to him be glory in the church and in Christ Jesus to all generations, forever and ever. Amen.

Ephesians 3:20–21

When Paul wrote to the Christians in Corinth he spoke of the unimaginable power of God at work in their lives too:

But, as it is written,
"What no eye has seen, nor ear heard,
nor the human heart conceived,
what God has prepared for those who love him" –
these things God has revealed to us through the Spirit; for the Spirit searches everything, even the depths of God.

1 Corinthians 2:9–10; cf. Isaiah 64:4

The Bible is clear that God is able to do far more than we can ever think of or dream of. So, if that is true, why don't you ask God to saturate your imagination? Why don't you ask him right now to enlarge your capacity to dream, to imagine, to think? If he is always bigger than our imaginations (and he has to be because he created them), then it is obvious, isn't it, that the bigger our imaginations become, the bigger we will understand God to be. We cannot out-think him. We cannot outsmart him. We cannot out-imagine him.

Saturated, sated, stirred, stretched

What is the impact of a saturated imagination? What could God do with us if we could only catch a bigger vision and picture of him? The answers are, well, they are unimaginable!

When Jesus was asked about the centre of life and faith, he responded with what we have come to call "The Great Commandment":

> " 'You must love the LORD your God with all your
> heart, all your soul, and all your mind.' This is
> the first and greatest commandment. A second is
> equally important: 'Love your neighbor as yourself.'
> The entire law and all the demands of the prophets
> are based on these two commandments."

Jesus speaking to a Pharisee, Matthew 22:37–40 (NLT)

We read these words through the lens of our own culture and therefore assume that to love the Lord with *all our heart* is the same as loving him with all of our emotions. That is not what *the heart* meant in Jewish culture. Those listening to Jesus speaking these words would have realized that he was quoting from the Torah, the Jewish Law. The words can be found in Deuteronomy 6:5 and Leviticus 19:18. Jewish thinking understood the heart to be the seat of the will and the intention. The bowels and the gut were the seat of emotion. So when Jesus told the Pharisees that they were to love the Lord their God with all their heart and all their soul and all their strength, he was saying something quite different from what we often assume.

Firstly, he told them that this love of God demands *complete* abandonment. Three times he says "all": love God with *all* your heart, with *all* your soul, and with *all* your mind. There are no half measures here. To follow God, we throw our all into it. Everything.

Secondly, Jesus started with the will and with the intention of the listener, not with the emotion. Love is not simply an emotion here; it is an act of the will. Love is a decision. If we wait until we *feel* like it, there will always be a reason for not loving God. There will be someone or something else that requires our attention and needs our time. It is when we *decide* to love God that we can then surrender our souls and our minds to him completely. The intention of the heart is a deeply important thing. Where our heart is determines where our focus is. Whatever captures our heart captures our life. That is not just about our emotions; it is about our will and our intentions. If you want to know the power that a decision of the heart has, just look at what changes in a teenager when they fall in love! They suddenly become aware of their appearance. They suddenly lose interest in the computer game that previously absorbed their attention. When someone captivates their heart, their whole life is affected.

The great Scottish Divine, Thomas Chalmers, preached a remarkable sermon that was published in 1855. It is entitled "The Expulsive Power of a New Affection". In it, Chalmers argues that it is not enough to tell people that they need forgiveness and that they have broken the laws and statutes of a Holy God. He tells his listeners and readers that it is only the ascendant power of a second affection that can drive out lesser affections. He argues that no exposition, however powerful or forcible, can bring about a lasting change of affections and desires in a human heart. Of course he is right! The love of God and the love of the world cannot exist for long in the same human heart. A love of God that captivates our hearts will drive out everything else because that is what the love of God does. It is when we surrender our heart to God – our will and intentions and decisions – that everything else follows.

Of course, we will still fall and stumble. We will still make mistakes, but when we surrender our will to the Lord Jesus Christ, we have surrendered the most powerful part of our life. We have handed him the keys to the car and we have agreed to become a passenger. We have stepped out of the circle of our own life. We have allowed ourselves to be led. This changes everything.

When we love the Lord with all of our heart, we love him with all of our will and all of our intentions and all of our desires. When we love him with all of our soul, we love him with all of our spiritual lives and all of our personality and all of our passion and all of our purpose. When we love him with all of our mind, then we are loving him with all of our intellect and all of our thoughts and all of our creativity. This is what it means to truly love God with all of ourselves.

What is another way of saying this?

Firstly, it is to say that we love God with all of our appetite and yearning – we hunger and we thirst for him. Nothing else will satisfy us. Nothing else will do. We have tasted him and we know that he is good (Psalm 34:8). We have come to realize that he is the only one who can satisfy our thirst. That is why the cry of the God gazer is that we want to look at God, to be caught up with him to such an extent that our imagination is saturated. When our imagination is saturated, our thirst will be sated. It is as we gaze at God and engage with him that we come to experience the reality that God is the food and drink in the best meal we will ever have (Matthew 5:6, *The Message*).

Secondly, as our thirst is sated, we realize that our passion is now stirred. One of the most intriguing things about Christian faith is that it is only as we follow that we deepen our relationship with God. God calls us to engage with him, not just to observe him. His is the voice that speaks to us. His is the breath that fills us. It is as we follow him that we become more passionate for him. It is as he pursues us that we become pursuers of him. The more we engage with God and allow him to engage with us, the deeper our passions are stirred and the greater our longing for him.

Thirdly, it is as we set our mind to him that we realize we will never get to the bottom of him. One of the most wonderful things about Christianity is that the further we go in our relationship with God, the more childlike we can become. It's a wonderfully liberating reality that the more we examine God, the less we know about him. This is not an increase in ignorance, however; it is more like an epiphany or a realization that there is so much more to him than we could ever imagine or think (there's that phrase from Ephesians 3 again!).

I have been a follower of Jesus Christ for almost thirty years and I am more in love with him now than I have ever been. I understand him less than I have ever understood him, but I trust him more than I ever have. Of course, I can explain lots of things about God, but my goodness, those facts are just snippets. Knowing him has transformed my life. I do not mean knowing *about* him; I mean *knowing* him. Knowing that he is here has changed the way I view my circumstances. Knowing that he cares has changed the way I care. Knowing that I can trust him has changed how I feel about the situations that I face. It is as he saturates our lives that we find our thirst sated, our passion stirred, and our intellect stretched. Good theology always results in deeper worship. Good theology always leaves us breathless and hopeful. Good theology always makes the greatness and the glory and the majesty of God greater, more glorious, and more majestic. Good theology causes us to gasp in wonder, to open our eyes in childlike amazement, and to blink with anticipation. Good theology stretches us and draws us in. It causes us to yearn for God, to reach out for him, to follow him. Good theology always pushes us beyond the boundaries of ourselves and leaves us with the deep, deep longing that others might know the God that we have come to know, because we know that in him is life.

A yearning that yearns for others to be free

The second part of Jesus' answer to the Pharisees in Matthew 22 was that we are to love our neighbour as we love ourselves. Love for God – genuine love for God – always changes the way we view ourselves and the way we view others. God gazers are not simply infatuated with God. We don't ignore the world around us. We don't pretend it isn't there. God gazers love God and come to love themselves because they know that God loves them. They take their identity, their meaning, and their purpose from what God says about them, but they do not lock themselves away from the world around them and pretend that they live in hermetically sealed units of glorious isolation. God gazers love others and yearn for them to be free.

When we have had a genuine encounter with God it results in us wanting to see other people changed by the same grace that has changed us. Our yearning becomes that other people might be free. We long to see people free from the limitations of a life without God. Our passion is that those who have been told that they are useless or worthless discover that they have a wonderful purpose and an inestimable value before God.

So much that we do as Christians could be seen as selfish, if we are not careful. Worship is not designed for us; it is designed for God. It is not supposed to make us feel good and happy and content with ourselves. Worship is for God. Worship and praise are directed towards him; they are *for* him. Two of the marks of genuine worship and praise are that we are drawn closer to God in intimacy and relationship, and that we are propelled into the world in service, mission, and proclamation of the gospel. The reality is that we cannot be God gazers and ignore the plight of men and women around us. We cannot be God gazers and refuse to serve. A selfish Christian is a contradiction in terms. God gazers care about society, they care about community, and they care about the truth. They cannot remain silent in the face of a decaying culture.

God gazers hunger and thirst for righteousness. God gazers seek God and pursue him. God gazers are never detached from the world in which they live or from the communities of which they are part. God gazers drink deeply from the wells of salvation (Isaiah 12:3), but they also want to share the water they have found because they yearn for people to see Christ, to hear Christ, and to encounter Christ. God gazers press into God.

A story is told of a man in the 1800s who lived more than a thousand miles away from Niagara Falls. The man had heard of the great Falls and decided to set out to see them for himself. He travelled on foot and his journey took many, many days. Towards the end of his journey he was, without realizing it, about seven miles away from Niagara Falls when he began to hear a rumbling, thunderous noise. He became excited and breathless, wondering if he was indeed close to his destination. As he continued walking, he passed a man who was mending the roof of a barn. The traveller called up to the man and asked if they could talk together for a moment. The farmer who was mending his barn roof came down to the traveller and they shared a glass of lemonade together. The traveller asked the man, "Can you tell me if that noise that I can hear in the distance is Niagara Falls?"

The farmer smiled back at the traveller and said, "Well, it could well be, but I can't be sure because I have never been."

God gazers walk the extra seven miles. They don't settle with the noise of the waterfall; they rush to the waterfall itself.

Don't allow yourself to be duped into thinking that a personal encounter with God through the power of the Holy Spirit is for everyone else. It is not. God wants to meet with *you*. God wants to encounter *you*. He wants to saturate *your* imagination. He wants to sate *your* thirst. He wants to stir *your* passion and he wants to stretch *your* intellect.

Shush. Can you hear something? Shush. I think I can hear it.

Is that the sound of thunder or is it the sound of a waterfall? Or maybe it's the sound of the God who yearns for intimacy with you far more than you can ever know.

Get off the roof of the barn. Stop what you are doing. Walk the extra seven miles. Meet God. You will never be the same again.

CHAPTER EIGHT

Not Just a Speaker but a Seeker

I want to be a God gazer!
Not a meetings manager
or a people pleaser
or a "tea and sympathy" vicar.
Not a leadership trainer.
Not just a speaker
but a seeker.

And without faith it is impossible to please God, for whoever would approach him must believe that he exists and that he rewards those who seek him.

Hebrews 11:6

Many pastors, teachers and preachers are frustrated. Many local church leaders are trapped in roles that they were never called to, doing things they do not like, desperately trying to function in gifts and skills that they have never been given. This situation arises when we ask people to come and lead our churches and then turn them into managers, administrators, and maintainers instead of releasing them to do the things that God has called them to do.

This is not a challenge that is just faced by church leaders; it is a challenge faced by any Christian when they find themselves trapped in a role they did not look for, and being squeezed by the impossible demands and expectations of others. We each need to find what we were made for and do it. Once you find that, you also find liberation in your heart and a freedom in your spirit. If you give your life to something you don't believe in, eventually you will lose your passion and your energy. If you give your life to something you believe in, then you can endure great hardships and great challenges because you know you are doing what you were born to do.

Are you doing what you were born for? Do you know what that is? Have you taken the time to find out? I pray you have. If you haven't, I pray you will.

By the way, there is nothing wrong with managers, administrators, and coordinators. Each of these wonderful gifts and roles and functions is beautiful. I am not arguing that everyone should be a pastor or a preacher or a church leader who teaches and does extraordinary things. I have already made the case for doing ordinary things in the extraordinary power of God. The point I want to make in this chapter is that each of us should discover what it is that God has called us to do, and do that.

Of course, there will be aspects of any role that we do not enjoy. We cannot haughtily refuse to do those things. It is incongruous and not Christlike to refuse to serve. There are times when we all have to do things that come with the territory of our wider roles.

The challenge – dare I say, the crisis – occurs when we end up giving all of our time and all of our energy to things that we do not feel gifted in, called to, or equipped for. Some churches are being led by people who are not called to lead churches. Some pulpits are occupied by people who have not been called to preach. Some people are cared for by people who are not called to be pastors. Some Christians are in jobs that do not suit their gifts and skills. We need to rediscover the art of seeking, of pressing in to God. We need to have a spirit that refuses to settle where God has not called us to settle, and a determination to find what God has called us to do, and then do it with all of our hearts.

Lessons from Moses

When Moses had led the Hebrew people out of Egypt, he found himself the leader of a people with problems. They had disputes that needed to be settled and grievances that needed to be heard. The task was becoming so great that it was wearing him down. He was sitting from morning until night hearing the claims and counterclaims of the Hebrews. Moses' father-in-law, Jethro, came to see him and discovered what he was doing. Jethro confronted Moses and told him that the ways things were being handled would not work and that Moses needed to find another solution. The story is told in Exodus 18:

> Moses' father-in-law replied, "What you are doing
> is not good. You and these people who come to
> you will only wear yourselves out. The work is too

> heavy for you; you cannot handle it alone. Listen
> now to me and I will give you some advice, and
> may God be with you."
>
> **Exodus 18:17–19 (NIV)**

Moses had allowed himself to fall into the trap of being defined by the expectations and demands of others. A similar situation arose when David, who would one day become king, volunteered to go and fight the giant Goliath. King Saul tried to put his own armour on the young boy. The armour didn't fit, however, and young David could not fight Goliath in Saul's armour:

> Saul said to David, "Go, and the LORD be with you."
> Then Saul dressed David in his own tunic. He put a
> coat of armour on him and a bronze helmet on his
> head. David fastened on his sword over the tunic
> and tried walking around, because he was not used
> to them.
> "I cannot go in these," he said to Saul, "because I
> am not used to them." So he took them off. Then
> he took his staff in his hand, chose five smooth
> stones from the stream, put them in the pouch of
> his shepherd's bag and, with his sling in his hand,
> approached the Philistine.
>
> **1 Samuel 17:37–40 (NIV)**

David was not created to wear Saul's armour, and he discovered that the moment he tried to please the king instead of being himself. Just like Moses, David needed to be himself; he needed to find a way of being the person that God had called him to be and not what everyone else expected him to be.

The same thing happened in the New Testament. In Acts 6, the early apostles had to think of a new way of serving the needs of the growing church in Jerusalem because they were becoming too absorbed in the wrong things to be doing the right things. Their job and responsibility was to give themselves to the Word of God and to prayer, but they were being drawn into things that could be done by others. They needed to focus on what God had called them to do and to be.

I think Peter allowed himself to be shaped by other peoples' expectations, too. Despite receiving a remarkable vision from God about a mission to the Gentiles in Acts 10, and despite being one of the leading proponents of the gospel breaking out of a strictly Jewish context in Acts 15, Peter allowed himself to be drawn into separatism and legalism again. It took the apostle Paul to challenge him about being what God had called him to be to actually shake Peter out of his wrong behaviour (Galatians 2).

In each situation, individuals had to make a choice to pursue what God wanted for their lives and not just what other people expected of them. They had to be seekers and not just people pleasers. You cannot be a people pleaser and a seeker of God at the same time.

Ask yourself whether these statements describe you in some situations:

- You try to be what someone else wants you to be even if you know it is not who you really are.

- You are afraid of the repercussions of saying something that will rock the boat, so you avoid doing so.

- You find it very hard to say what you want or to

be honest about how you feel for fear of upsetting someone.

- You avoid speaking your mind because you think it causes too much confrontation.

- You find it easier to go along with what someone wants or to fit into their opinion than to be honest about your concerns or your disagreements.

- You have dreams of working with someone who is strong enough to take over your decisions and make your job easier.

- You find it really hard to express your opinions to people who are close to you if you know that your opinion and theirs will clash.

- You find it really hard to say no to someone so you often do things even though you do not want to do them.

- You avoid getting angry.

- You do not like taking the initiative because you worry that it might be the wrong thing to do.

- You always try to be nice rather than expressing how you really feel.

- You want everyone to like you, and you will do almost anything to be popular or liked.

If these patterns of thought and behaviour are an accurate description of you, even if only in some situations or some relationships, then you are a people pleaser. This may not be your personality type, but it is your personality pattern. If these statements describe even a part of how you process decisions and do things, then it means that part of you seeks to be a people pleaser. If these descriptions define you most of the time, then you are most often a people pleaser. If these descriptions describe you all the time, then you are living to please other people all the time. Whichever category you fall into, you cannot simultaneously live to please people and live to please God. You have to make a choice.

What does people pleasing have to do with being a seeker?

Moses, David, the apostles in general, and Peter in particular all had to make a choice. So do we. We can *either* seek God's purpose for our lives and pursue it *or* we can seek to be popular and fit in with other people's expectations of us. Seeking God doesn't mean you will automatically upset everyone, by the way. Often, serving God and seeking his will for your life will win you the respect, admiration, and support of people around you – often, but not always. There are times when your decision to seek God and his kingdom first will be unpopular. As a preacher, you sometimes have to say hard things. As an employee, doing the right thing is not always the same as doing the easy thing. As a husband or a wife, you sometimes have to say the hard thing to your partner. As a parent, you are not always Mr or Mrs Popular!

The connection between doing what God has called you to do and not simply pleasing others is simply that if you want to be all that God wants you to be, then you must put him at the centre of your life. His must be the dominant voice, and his will must be the most important thing for you. Seekers recognize that God is the ultimate definer of their personhood, their purpose in life, and their place in the world. God gazers are seekers. They are people who want to be defined, determined, and discipled by what God says.

I lead a church where not just *one* but *two* of the previous senior pastors continue to be actively involved in the life of the church. It works wonderfully and I am deeply grateful to both Jim Graham and Stephen Gaukroger for their love, their support, and their counsel. It works because both of these men are seekers after God, and it works because I am, too. They do not seek to make me behave like them, and I do not seek to make them approve of me. I do not need their approval because I already have God's approval. God called me to lead Gold Hill, and God will sustain me in my leadership of Gold Hill. Jim and Stephen both recognize that their period of leadership at Gold Hill in a formal capacity has ended, and they have never once tried to control me or force me to do what they want. We don't always agree on everything, but I love these two men very deeply and appreciate their wisdom and their guidance. They influence me very deeply, but they do not own me. They are not my ultimate audience. Nor is the church family that I lead. God is the one whom I set out to please.

There are times when I have had to say difficult and challenging things to the church family, but that is because I am serving them *in Christ's name.* They may pay my salary cheque every month, but they do not own me. Jesus Christ owns me, and therefore he is the one whom I seek. Should there ever be a time when he asks me to move to a new sphere of ministry, then I should be ready to obey and follow him because I seek him first and foremost. Thankfully the church family and the leadership of Gold Hill are extremely supportive of this position. They are the most remarkable family to be a part of, and I thank God that he brought us together.

Are you a seeker? Is it your heart's deepest desire to be what God has called you to be and to do what God has called you to do? You may be a conference speaker, a preacher, a leadership trainer, a manager, a pastor, or the director of a company, but I am asking you: do you have the heart of a seeker? Do you seek, above everything else, to please God and to serve him? Whether you do that through volunteering in a school, publishing books, being a politician, running a business, or working for the government, is it your heart's desire to put him first and foremost and to seek his will above all things?

Seven simple principles concerning the art of seeking God

I guess there are many things that I could say about seeking after God. So many that several books could be written about these principles; indeed, many books *have* been written about this subject. I want to share with you just seven simple principles concerning the art of seeking God. They are straightforward and simple to understand but I trust that they will be helpful to you and provide you with some tools to help you in your pursuit of God and his purposes for your life.

There is always more of God for you to know

We can never get to the bottom of God. We can never explain him away. If you think about it, this is how it should be, because if we were ever in a position to explain God, then we would have made ourselves greater than him. David cried out in worship to God that God's thoughts were precious to David and that there were so many of them that they were more numerous than all the grains of sand on the earth (Psalm 139:17–18). God's greatness and vastness are more than the human heart can fathom (Psalm 139:6).

Voyager 1 was about to leave our solar system in 1990, having completed its mission. As it left, the scientists at NASA turned the spacecraft's camera around and took a photograph of the earth. It was taken from a distance of around 3.7 billion miles away. Carl Sagan, the astronomer and astrophysicist, called the picture the "Pale Blue Dot". The picture showed the earth about one tenth of a pixel in size, suspended in the vast emptiness of space. Sagan wrote:

> That's here. That's home. That's us. On it everyone you love, everyone you know, everyone you ever heard of, every human being who ever was, lived out their lives … on a mote of dust suspended in a sunbeam.[9]

Christianity teaches that the universe in all of its vastness was created by God, who is bigger than the universe (Psalm 19:1), more powerful than the most powerful forces of earth, and infinitely greater than anything we can conceive of. There is no one to whom we can compare him and nothing that can explain his greatness (Isaiah 40:25–26; Romans 1:20). Indeed, the German philosopher Friedrich Schiller once remarked that the universe was one of God's thoughts! Once we accept the premise of the greatness of

---

9   Carl Sagan, *Pale Blue Dot: A Vision of the Human Future in Space*, New York: Random House, 1994, p.6.

God, his utter vastness, there is almost an automatic desire to explore him. It is as we continually ponder him and his greatness that we become more and more amazed at his utter greatness. A God who can be confined, defined, or refined is too small. A God who can be domesticated is too tame. A God who can be relativized is too weak. A God who can be comprehended is too boring.

Refuse to become an expert or a professional

Professionalizing your pursuit of God is spiritual suicide. Never allow yourself to make your pursuit of God either a pastime or something that you do only because you are paid to do it or expected to do it. We see the antithesis of this attitude in the apostle Paul, who relentlessly pursued God. It was the great obsession of his life to pursue God and all that God had for him. Jesus told his disciples to seek God's kingdom above and beyond all things (Matthew 6:33). Seekers refuse to make God small, and they refuse to make him the means whereby they make a living.

Preachers and teachers must be cautious here above all other people. We do not approach the Bible simply to find a thought for a sermon, or the latest theological nicety to tickle the fancy of our listeners. We approach the Bible believing that in it we discover truths about God. These truths will change our lives, upset our presuppositions, demolish our prejudices, and force a rethinking of our most cherished worldviews. God is not contained in one branch of Christian theology. He is not a protestant or a catholic. He is above gender and above politics and above the small labels and boxes in which we attempt to confine him.

Make the face of God your delight; not just his hand

Seekers do not simply come to God for what they can get. They seek him so that they might know him better. They do not simply seek the things that he can do for them, the things he can give them. They seek intimacy with him. They seek deeper relationship with him. They seek a greater encounter with him. Whether that seeker is David (Psalm 27:8) or the apostle Paul (Philippians 3), their desire is not simply to know more *about* God; their desire is to *know* God more.

There is a prayer, attributed to Ambrose of Milan, which expresses beautifully this desire to seek God's face:

> O Lord,
> teach me to seek you,
> and reveal yourself to me
> when I seek you.
>
> For I cannot seek you unless
> you first teach me,
> nor find you unless
> you first reveal yourself to me.
>
> Let me seek you in longing,
> and long for you in seeking.
>
> Let me find you in love,
> and love you in finding.

Ambrose of Milan, c. 340–397. (See also the end of Chapter 1 of Anselm's Proslogion)[10]

10 Accessed at www.sdc.me.uk/pray/seeking_the_Lord.html (accessed 28 November 2014). The Societas Doctrinae Christianae is a society of lay catechesis that began in Malta in 1907 and provides a number of resources for those seeking to develop their prayer life and their spirituality. See also Sidney D. Deane (trans.) "*Proslogion*" *St Anselm: Basic Writings*, Chicago: Open Court, 1962.

We must always remember that God is not playing hide-and-seek with us. He wants to be found by us. He created us for fellowship with himself (Genesis 1–3) and he longs for us to walk in intimacy with him. He invites us to seek him (Isaiah 55:6), and the Lord Jesus encourages his disciples to have a persistent and purposeful attitude of seeking the Holy Spirit and the power of God (Matthew 7:7; Luke 11:13). We far too often come to God in order to get something from him, as if he were a great slot machine or benefactor. Yet the heart of Christian faith is not seeking him in order to get something but instead seeking him for the pleasure of his company. It is in his company that we find ourselves, it is in close fellowship with him that we find who we really are, and it is as we spend time with him, walking with him and listening to him, that we discover the grace and the power to be truly alive and truly free (Matthew 11:28–30). To seek God's face is to seek a fuller revelation of who he is and to be willing to turn from everything that will get in the way of that revelation (2 Chronicles 7:14).

Can there be anything more beautiful and more life giving than the face of God? Is there anything more wonderful, more releasing, and more enabling than spending time with the one who upholds all things by his powerful word (Hebrews 1)? No wonder John the apostle, as an old man, could speak with such eloquence and depth about God. He had spent time with him, he had walked with him, he had gazed deeply into God's face as he gazed at the face of Christ (1 John 1). To seek God's face is to make him our delight and our joy:

> Trust in the LORD, and do good;
> dwell in the land and befriend faithfulness.
> Delight yourself in the LORD,
> and he will give you the desires of your heart.
> Commit your way to the LORD;
> trust in him, and he will act.
> He will bring forth your righteousness as the light,
> and your justice as the noonday.

Psalm 37:3–6 (ESV)

We not only take delight in the Lord by deliberately and intentionally spending time with him and focusing on him; we also delight in him by choosing to live in a way that he has commended to us and in which he has commanded us to walk:

> "If you turn back your foot from the Sabbath,
> from doing your pleasure on my holy day,
> and call the Sabbath a delight
> and the holy day of the LORD honourable;
> if you honour it, not going your own ways,
> or seeking your own pleasure, or talking idly;
> then you shall take delight in the LORD,
> and I will make you ride on the heights of the earth;
> I will feed you with the heritage of Jacob your father,
> for the mouth of the LORD has spoken."

Isaiah 58:13–14 (ESVUK)

The prophet Isaiah found great delight in the Lord. He had discovered the great secret of joy and purpose and meaning and contentment. These things only come to us as we seek God's face and heart; not just his hand. That is why Isaiah could cry out:

> I delight greatly in the LORD;
> my soul rejoices in my God.
> For he has clothed me with garments of salvation
> and arrayed me in a robe of righteousness,
> as a bridegroom adorns his head like a priest,
> and as a bride adorns herself with her jewels.

Isaiah 61:10 (NIV)

As part of the bride, we now delight ourselves in our groom, Jesus. Our delight in him is like jewels in our garments – what a beautiful picture. In his reflections on the psalms, C. S. Lewis articulates the wonderful truth of the power of delighting in the Lord:

> I think we delight to praise what we enjoy because
> the praise not merely expresses but completes the
> enjoyment; it is its appointed consummation. It is
> not out of compliment that lovers keep on telling
> one another how beautiful they are; the delight
> is incomplete until it is expressed … If it were
> possible for a created soul fully … to "appreciate",
> that is to love and delight in, the worthiest object
> of all, and simultaneously at every moment to give
> delight perfect expression, then that soul would be
> in supreme beatitude … The Scotch catechism says
> that man's chief end is "to glorify God and enjoy
> him forever." But we shall then know that these
> are the same thing. Fully to enjoy is to glorify. In
> commanding us to glorify Him, God is inviting us to
> enjoy Him.[11]

---

11 C. S. Lewis, *Reflections on the Psalms: The Celebrated Musings on One of the Most Intriguing Books of the Bible*, London: Harvest Books/Harcourt In, 1986, p.95.

You cannot lead others to places
where you have not been

There is no doubt that you cannot lead people into the presence of God if you are unable to go there yourself. This reality is seen supremely in the Lord Jesus himself, of course. He has entered the very presence of God on our behalf, and by doing so he has enabled us to come boldly into that very place ourselves (Hebrews 4:16). It is because Christ has gone ahead of us that we can now enter the very presence of God.

We cannot push people into new places with God; instead we have to pull them. By that I mean that we must first be *drawn* into God's presence ourselves, and then encourage other people to join us there (John 6:44). Now I know that God's presence is everywhere and that there is nowhere we can go where God is not. I am not talking about that general theological truth here, nor am I trying to decry the ordinary lives we live. Rather, I am trying to elevate them both. We can press into the felt and experienced presence of God in the very midst of our ordinary lives.

Those who seek to live perpetually with an awareness of the presence of God are like magnets to other people. Those around us are attracted to Christlikeness in us. They are inexplicably drawn towards Christ because Christ has said that when he is lifted up he will draw all people to himself. Those who seek to honour the presence of God in their lives love truth, they love others, they honour righteousness, they value commitments and relationships, and they value other people.

We cannot take others where we ourselves have not been. If we yearn to walk in the sensed presence of God, if we seek after him, then we will practise spending time in his presence ourselves. If we yearn for God's presence, then we will deliberately and intentionally praise and worship God because God inhabits the praises of his people (Psalm 22:3). We will fix our eyes on Jesus and on what he is doing in the world and in our lives (Hebrews 12:1–2). As Christians, we so often want to see people go further in God, to enable them to understand more of his grace and love for their lives. If that is what we want, then we ourselves must learn what it is to enjoy the Lord and seek his presence. Nothing will dissuade people of the truth of Christ more than a person who says that they believe in Jesus but whose life does not display that same commitment.

This is about all of who you are, not just a part of who you are

Seekers have recognized that pursuing God is about laying our whole lives before him, and not just those parts that we are comfortable with laying down. One of the greatest blights on Christianity in Europe and North America is the way we have divided it into "sacred" and "secular" categories. There is no such division. All of our lives matter to God. Seekers know that this is true, and they lay their whole lives before God.

We need God's grace and a refilling of his Spirit as often as we need to breathe

Seekers recognize that we are dependent upon God for every single physical breath. We understand that all life flows from God, and we are grateful for the gift of every moment, but we also recognize something more. Our spiritual vitality and capacity is dependent upon a constant refilling of the Holy Spirit. We understand the truth of Jesus' words that without him we can do nothing (John 15).

As someone who was converted in a Pentecostal church, I have always been very aware of the command of Paul to the Christians in Ephesus, that they should continually be filled with the Holy Spirit (Ephesians 5:18). I have heard this command taught in a way that expects people to be filled with the Holy Spirit every week or every day. I do not think that goes far enough. We are to be filled with the Holy Spirit as often as we are to be filled with physical breath. Every single breath we breathe is a gift from God. Indeed, we are reminded that God holds every one of our breaths in his hand (Job 12:10). The Hebrew word is translated as both "spirit" and "breath", and the same is true for the Greek. It is valid to translate "Holy Spirit" as "Holy Breath".

Just as you and I need God's gift of physical breath every single time we inhale and exhale, so it is true that we need to be continually and repeatedly filled with the Holy Spirit in order to live our lives for the glory of God. We cannot survive with gulps of air once a week. We must try not to hold our breath from one Sunday to another or from one small group meeting to another. We must learn the art of practising the presence of God. It is a wonderful release to remember that God is constantly with us, constantly filling us, constantly sustaining us. Somehow it changes the pressure that we feel. We are never dependent upon ourselves. God never tells us to get on with it without his help. Such ideas point towards human self-sufficiency far too much.

Our great challenge is that we have turned the Holy Spirit into someone who helps us along and enables us to get things right when we need a bit of support. This is not at all the idea of the Spirit's presence and power in our lives. Chapters 14–16 of John's Gospel shows him to be *the One called alongside to help*, but to make this mean that he helps us when we need his help is to miss the point entirely. He helps us with *everything* because we *always* need his help. We are not capable of getting it right without his help. Of course, we may be able to be nice or kind or loving for a little while in our own strength, but we will never achieve anything of eternal worth and value without his *constant* presence and *constant* refilling. We have made the power and presence of God a "top-me-up", when it is actually a vital lifeline and support. Seekers know this. We know that we are utterly and completely dependent upon his grace and his power, because we know that without God we will end up pleasing people and doing the wrong thing.

God wants to encounter you far more than you want to encounter God

This is the last key principle I want to leave with you as a seeker. God longs for intimacy with us far more than we long for intimacy with him. He made us for this purpose.

He waits for us. We do not need to be anxious about whether God wants us to seek him. From the beginning of the Bible to the end, he invites us to pursue him.

God loved us long before we loved him. He waits for us to turn and seek him, and when we do, we will find him. This is the great paradox of Christian faith: it is as we pursue God that we discover he has been pursuing us all along. He has been waiting to be found by us. He will not force himself upon us, but he does not run from us. Like the father in Luke 15 who waits for his son to return, he is looking for us. He knows our walk; he is familiar with our gait. He is ready to run to us, embrace us, and restore us to relationship with himself. His invitation echoes throughout time and history, and his heartbeat is felt with every breath. He longs for intimacy with us.

These seven simple principles will help us in the art of seeking God. There is always more of God to know. We must never allow ourselves to become experts or professionals in the art of seeking God. It is as we make seeking God's face our delight that we will discover him most powerfully. We will never lead others to a place where we have not been. Our whole lives matter to God, and it is as we surrender everything to him that we discover the richness of his presence and power in our lives. We need the constant presence of the Spirit and his power in our lives. God wants to encounter us far more than we want to encounter him.

God gazers know that God has made them for a purpose. They will not become pale imitations of what they were born to be. They will seek God with all their hearts. They will open their whole lives to the presence of

God. They will not allow themselves to become the pawns in someone else's game. It is God and God alone whom they seek. Their desire is to be what God has called them to be because they know that it is only as they live out their destiny before God that they can be truly alive and truly happy.

Don't let yourself be determined by your circumstances. Don't allow yourself to become absorbed into someone else's definition of who you are. My dear brother and sister, fix your eyes on Christ, the Author and Finisher of your faith, and allow yourself to make this one simple resolution: say to God, *"Lord, whatever you have for me, give, and whatever you want of me, I will give it."*

Above everything, before anything, seek God.

Put him first.

You will not be disappointed.

CHAPTER NINE

God, Gaze Through Me

I want to be a God gazer...
and for a moment I want God
to gaze through me.
I want others to see
his Eyes,
Heart,
Mind,
and Love
above everything else in me.

G od is most glorified in us when we are most delighted in him. In other words, if the central motivation of our lives has become the glory of God and his name, then the central aim of our lives will be to do what pleases him, and pleasing him will become our greatest satisfaction. It is as we love him that we find ourselves loving others more deeply. That is because as we love him, he releases his love not only *to* us but also *through* us to other people. In fact, the Bible makes it very clear that if we truly love God, then we will inevitably love other people, too. It is the deep desire of the God gazer that when others look at his or her life, they will see the love of God looking back. Not only that, but the God gazer also knows that love always looks like *something*.

Whom should I love?

There is simplicity in understanding which people we should love, according to the teaching of the Bible. It may not be difficult to explain, but it is incredibly hard to do in our own strength. Let me turn my attention to which people I should love.

I want to take a moment and think about Jesus' words in the Great Commandment once again, but this time we shall explore the words that Luke records about what Jesus said:

> Just then a lawyer stood up to test Jesus. "Teacher," he said, "what must I do to inherit eternal life?" He said to him, "What is written in the law? What do you read there?" He answered, "You shall love the Lord your God with all your heart, and with all your soul, and with all your strength, and with all your mind; and your neighbour as yourself." And he said to him, "You have given the right answer; do this, and you will live."

Luke 10:25–28

Now there are several things about this little portion of Luke's Gospel of which we should take special note. Firstly, the Pharisee asked the question to try and catch Jesus out, which means that his motive was not entirely pure, although that does not matter for the sake of our conversation. Secondly, we see that the Pharisee wanted to know how to inherit eternal life. He wanted to know what he should believe in order to enjoy the promise of eternal life. As we will see, the answer that Jesus gave, via the mouth of the Pharisee himself, was a much fuller description of belief than the Pharisee wanted to hear.

When Jesus asked the Pharisee to tell Jesus what the law said in answer to the question, "What must I do to inherit eternal life?" the Pharisee quoted Deuteronomy 6. This is a part of the Torah that Jews repeated twice a day, so it is no wonder that he was able to answer so eloquently. The Pharisee knew what the law said. He knew that the Torah said a Jew was to love the Lord their God with all their heart and all their soul and all their strength and all their mind. The Pharisee also knew that this had been elaborated to include loving their neighbour as they loved themselves.

Did you notice the crucial response of Jesus at the end of the little exchange? Jesus said, "You have given the right answer; *do this* and you will live." I've added the emphasis so you catch what I am trying to say. The Pharisee knew what the answer was, but he was missing the point. To believe this is not a matter of reciting it twice a day. To believe this is to *do* it. You do not believe what you do not put into practice. Jesus told the Pharisee to love the Lord, to love his neighbour, and to love himself.

The Pharisee went on to ask for a definition of whom his neighbour was, evoking Jesus' famous parable about the Good Samaritan (Luke 10:29–37). Jesus told the Pharisee that his neighbour was anyone who was close to him and had a need that the Pharisee saw, even if that person were a member of a group as deeply suspected and rejected as the Samaritans. That would have been as startling to the Pharisee as it is to us today. It is the equivalent of Jesus telling Serbs that Croatians were their neighbours, or Jesus telling Irish Protestants that Catholics were their neighbours. It would be like Jesus telling Sunnis in Iraq that Shias were their neighbours and that they should love them.

The point I want to make from these verses is whom Jesus tells the Pharisee to love. There are three parts to the answer:

- He must love God.

- He must love himself.

- He must love his neighbour.

Having looked at the words of Jesus recorded in Luke 10:25–37, let us explore a second Scripture. In the encounter recorded in Matthew 5–7, known as the Sermon on the Mount, Jesus was speaking to his disciples and setting out a radical new way of living and thinking for them that flowed out of the Torah but deeply challenged the way they had been taught. Having told them that he had come to fulfil the law and not to destroy or remove it (Matthew 5:17–20), Jesus went on to talk about the way they should approach sexual purity, marriage and divorce, their use of words and promises, retaliation, and lastly how they were to respond to enemies. It is the last section of what he said that I want to think about – namely how they should approach their enemies.

> "You have heard that it was said, 'You shall love
> your neighbour and hate your enemy.' But I say to
> you, Love your enemies and pray for those who
> persecute you, so that you may be children of

> your Father in heaven; for he makes his sun rise
> on the evil and on the good, and sends rain on the
> righteous and on the unrighteous. For if you love
> those who love you, what reward do you have?
> Do not even the tax-collectors do the same? And
> if you greet only your brothers and sisters, what
> more are you doing than others? Do not even the
> Gentiles do the same? Be perfect, therefore, as your
> heavenly Father is perfect."

Matthew 5:43–48

So here we have another aspect of Jesus' teaching. In the Sermon on the Mount he commanded his disciples to love their enemies, not to hate them. As far as I understand it, then, the teaching of Jesus gives us four groups of people whom we must love:

- We must love God.

- We must love ourselves.

- We must love our neighbour.

- We must love our enemy.

That is straightforward. Now, let me ask you a question. Who do you know anywhere on planet earth who does not fall into one of these categories?

Is there anyone excluded?

Anyone?

I didn't think so.

So when it comes to people, we are to love them. Full stop. No caveats. No riders. No get-out clauses. Now, of course, that does not mean that we are to love the structures of evil or the forces of darkness. We are to love not the world (system) or the things of the world (1 John 2:15). We are to hate sin and evil (Psalm 97:10; Proverbs 8:13). But we are to love people.

As I said, that is easy to understand but it is incredibly difficult to live out, yet we are left with the fundamental challenge that love always looks like something. Jesus' words to the Pharisee are his words to us: we are to *do* this. John makes it very clear that we cannot say that we love God and hate our brother (1 John 4:20), and James makes it clear that our faith is evidenced in our love of the poor and the excluded (James 2:14–16).

Love always looks like something.

Always.

That means that if I am a God gazer and I love God, then that will be evidenced in my life. When other people look at me they will see in me a love for God, a love for myself, a love for my neighbour, and a love for my enemies. God will not love me *because* these things are evidenced; rather it is *because* God loves me that these things will be evidenced. If they are not, there is something wrong with the way I understand love.

Love always looks like something.

Always.

How are you doing in this area?

God, gaze through me

I want to be a God gazer...
and for a moment I want God
to gaze through me.
I want others to see
his Eyes,

Heart,
Mind,
and Love
above everything else in me.

That just has to be the cry of every Christian on the planet, doesn't it? That God would be seen in us is the greatest privilege and the deepest honour imaginable. Somehow, we want people to see Jesus in us. It happened to Peter and John in Acts 4 as they stood before the ruling Jewish Council, the Sanhedrin:

> When they saw the courage of Peter and John and realized that they were unschooled, ordinary men, they were astonished and they took note that these men had been with Jesus.
>
> **Acts 4:13 (NIV)**

Somehow the leaders in Jerusalem, who could not verify the miracle that had just happened in the man who had been healed outside the temple (look at Acts 4:14), were able to see something different in Peter and John. They saw their boldness. They had just heard Peter tell them, the leaders of Israel, that Jesus was the *only* name through which salvation would come. They had heard Peter and John refuse to deny their faith. They saw their boldness and they took note of it.

As I write these words, there are Christians being martyred in the Middle East, North Korea, Nigeria and Somalia, to name but a few countries. The World Watch list names the top fifty countries where Christians are being persecuted for their faith. The most dangerous place to be a Christian right now is North Korea, followed by Somalia, Syria, Iraq, Afghanistan, and Saudi Arabia. It lists fourteen countries where extreme persecution is taking place, thirteen countries where severe persecution is taking place and twenty-two countries where moderate persecution is taking place.[12] I have no doubt that in these countries, where my brothers and sisters are facing persecution or even death, God is gazing through them. Despite their terrible circumstances and the unpredictability of their futures, God is gazing through them.

Is it our prayer that God would gaze through us? Is it our deepest longing that others would see Christ in us? Peter told the church that they were a chosen people, a royal priesthood, a holy nation, God's special people *that they might declare the praises of him who called them out of darkness and into his wonderful light* (1 Peter 2:9). Paul could urge the Corinthians to follow him because he was following Christ (1 Corinthians 11:1). He could also urge Timothy and Titus to follow his example. Paul could tell Philemon that Philemon could trust Paul to settle Onesimus' debt when Paul saw Philemon again. The book of Acts is full of examples of the power of the witness of the early church (Acts 2 and Acts 4 are just two examples). When Jesus spoke to the churches in Revelation 1–3, he commented on the power of some of their faith and their testimony. The saints of the Old Testament left examples in their lives of their faithfulness to God, too. People saw what they believed in the way they lived.

Surely it is the prayer of all Christians everywhere that people might see Christ in us, that they might catch a

---

12 Via Open Doors UK, http://www.opendoorsuk.org/persecution/country_profiles. php (accessed 12 November 2014).

glimpse of the grace and love and mercy of God in our lives?

How do people see God in us?

There are obvious ways in which people see God in us. The early church demonstrated the love of God to those around them by the way they loved one another. Paul told the Galatian Christians to do good to all, especially to those who were of the household of faith (Galatians 6:10; Matthew 25).

Aristides, sent by the Roman Emperor Hadrian to spy on the strange people known as "Christians", returned to Hadrian with a mixed report of the Christians he had witnessed, yet his words echo still as a challenge to those of us who are Christians: *"Behold how they love one another!"* Jesus told his disciples that their love would be demonstrated to the world by whether or not they were willing to lay down their lives for one another (John 15:13). He, of course, demonstrated his love by living and dying for us. Even before we loved him, he loved us (1 John 4). Paul told the Roman Christians that God demonstrated his love for us by sending Jesus to die for us before we had any love at all for God (Romans 5:6–8). People will see God in us when we are willing to suffer and to die for our brothers, our sisters, and our God. They will see the love of God in us when we are willing to put the needs and the well-being of other people before our own. The powerful witness of service and love and devotion in our lives shines out the love of God to other people.

Others will see the love of God in our *attitudes*. The way we approach life in general, the core values by which we live, and the way we make decisions about how we treat people will display the love of God to those around us (Matthew 5).

People around us will also see the love of God in our *lifestyle*. The choices we make, the way we handle money and material possessions and things display where our heart is (Matthew 6).

Our love of God will shine out in our *actions*, in the way we treat the poor, the marginalized, and the excluded. If we ignore the cries of the poor, how can we be following the Jesus who leads us to the poor? Our faith is evidenced in the way we treat the vulnerable and the excluded, whether that means serving them (Isaiah 58, Matthew 25:31–46), challenging the structures that exclude them (Proverbs 31:8), becoming an advocate for justice and fairness (Amos 5), or welcoming them into our families, our homes, and our churches (James 2).

People will also see the love of God in us when they see that our *priorities* reflect the priorities of Jesus. When we allow his teaching to shape us and when we seek to do his will (John 15); when we are willing to take up a cross and follow him (Mark 8:34–38); when we are willing to be associated with him instead of being embarrassed by him (1 Samuel 2:30; John 12:26); and when we are willing to be fearless in our proclamation of the gospel that he died for our sins according to the Scriptures and that he was buried and that he rose again on the third day (1 Corinthians 15:1–3).

Our society and our loved ones and those around us will see Christ in us when our *relationships* reflect the values and the heart of Jesus too (Matthew 7) – when we judge other people with grace and gentleness, and when we apply an attitude of forgiveness and restoration to others in the way that God has applied those things to us.

The fruit of the Spirit in our lives produce a visible expression of the love of God to others: love, joy, peace, patience, kindness, goodness, faithfulness gentleness and self-control. Paul tells us that when these things are evidenced in our lives they have a deep impact, and against such things there is no law (Galatians 5:22–23).

We also demonstrate the love of God in preaching the gospel of Jesus Christ (Romans 1:16) and in being fearless in our willingness to pray for the sick, raise the dead, confront the powers of the devil, and declare the presence and power of the kingdom of God (Matthew 10; 12; 28:16–20; Mark 16; Acts 1; 1 Corinthians 2:4).

These are powerful *evidences* or *demonstrations* of the love of God to the world around us: our attitudes; our lifestyle; our actions; our priorities; our relationships; the depth and strength of our character; our willingness to remain faithful to Jesus and to the message of his gospel; our readiness to serve the broken, the poor, and the excluded; our willingness to engage in the mission of God in the world around us; our willingness to suffer for our faith; our willingness to preach the gospel, heal the sick, raise the dead, confront the powers of the devil, and demonstrate the power of God and the presence of his kingdom. All of these things demonstrate and display the love of God to the world around us.

Our friends, our families, and our world need to see people who are passionately in love with God. They need to see the love of God through us and in us. We know this as Christians, yet we find it very hard to let God's love shine through us. Maybe that is because we have forgotten that we are cracked vessels from whom the love and grace of God shine out (2 Corinthians 4). Maybe it is because we are afraid of the vulnerability and frailty that comes from being broken: after all, a vessel that is cracked is a vessel that is broken, isn't it? Maybe it is because vulnerability demands dependence, and we do not like being dependent?

I could give many reasons for us finding it hard to let the love of God shine from us and through us, but there is one that I want to focus in on: perhaps we're trying too hard to do God's work for him and we are not letting him do his work through us?

Giving Christ our lives

We have forgotten that if we want the world to see Christ in us, we have to see the world through Christ's eyes. If we want the world to experience his heart in us, we have to be willing to feel his heart for the world. If we want people to hear the reasoning and the mind of Christ in us, we have to be willing to have the mind of Christ. If we want his life to be experienced through us, we must first experience his life in us. If we want him to be seen above everything in us, we have to be willing to subordinate everything in our lives to him. In the words of John the Baptist, Jesus' cousin, Jesus must increase in importance and I must decrease in importance (John 3:30). I think it was Hudson Taylor who once said that anyone can be a committed Christian – all it takes is our lives.

As we approach the end of this first section of *God Gazer*, it is worth taking a moment to reflect on what we have thought about so far.

God gazers are captured by the utter beauty and magnitude of God. We see him in the ordinary, everyday moments of our lives. We meet him in the here and the now. We do not look to recreate some kind of shimmering past history; instead we believe that the best is yet to be and that God is present today to meet with us and to transform us. We do not make judgments of one another or of ourselves according to the world's measure of success and achievement; instead we seek to see people as God sees them and to treat them as God would treat them. We are desperate for God, not for more religion, and we are deeply convinced of the goodness and the graciousness and the gentleness of God. We want to grow in the grace of God, to discover new things about him, and we want our passions to be stirred and our thinking to be stretched because we know there is so much more of God to discover.

Now imagine a local church that garners all these attributes. Imagine a small band of people who are relentlessly pursuing all that God is and all that God has for them. Imagine what that community would *feel* like. Imagine what it would talk about. Imagine where its priorities would lie and what its core values would be like. Imagine being part of a community where the broken are welcome, where people are encouraged to flourish, where the truth is told, where the presence of Jesus is tangible, where the Holy Spirit has free rein to do what he wants, when he wants, with whom he wants. Imagine a community of faith so committed to its neighbourhood that the neighbourhood would grieve if the church were to close. Imagine a church that believes that its future is brighter than its past, a church that is not ashamed of Jesus. Imagine a church where people come to be prayed for, a community that is open twenty-four hours a day, seven days a week, where imperfect people are perfectly welcome. Imagine a group of Christians who have not given up on God because they know that God has not given up on them. Imagine a church family that is willing to be authentic, willing to be vulnerable, willing to share life with one another in all of its glorious beauty and its deep despair. Imagine a church where everyone matters, where there is no hierarchy of importance, and where everyone can play their part, make a difference, and support one another. Imagine a church family that wants to be authentic in its worship, real in its relationships, and wants to encounter God, make disciples, and change the world.

That's the kind of church I want to be a part of.

What about you?

That kind of church would be alive, vibrant, connected. It would attract people. It would give hope to people. It would change its community and the world. It would bring life and vitality to all those who come into contact with it.

That's the thing, you see.

When you are a God gazer, the inevitable consequence is that you want to be a life giver. The one leads to the other.

> I want to be a God gazer!
> Captured by the brilliance
> that springs from the radiance
> of you.

SECTION TWO

"Life Givers"

The inevitable consequence of an encounter with God

Wherever the river goes, every living creature that swarms will live, and there will be very many fish, once these waters reach there. It will become fresh; and everything will live where the river goes ...
On the banks, on both sides of the river, there will grow all kinds of trees for food. Their leaves will not wither nor their fruit fail, but they will bear fresh fruit every month, because the water for them flows from the sanctuary. Their fruit will be for food, and their leaves for healing.

Ezekiel's Vision of the River of Life, Ezekiel Chapter 47, Verses 9, 12 (cf. Revelation 22:1–2)

"Oh, Eeyore, you are wet!" said Piglet, feeling him. Eeyore shook himself, and asked somebody to explain to Piglet what happened when you had been inside a river for quite a long time.

A. A. Milne, Winnie-the-Pooh

CHAPTER TEN

I Want My Life to Be Releasing

I want to be a Life giver
not a life sucker.
I want my life to be releasing,
not appeasing or placating.

Jesus said to her, "Everyone who drinks of this
water will be thirsty again, but those who drink of
the water that I will give them will never be thirsty.
The water that I will give will become in them a
spring of water gushing up to eternal life." The
woman said to him, "Sir, give me this water, so that
I may never be thirsty or have to keep coming here
to draw water."

A dialogue between Jesus and a woman at a well, John 4:13–15

There is something wonderful about seeing other people grow. I like nothing more than to watch someone gain confidence in who they are in Christ and grow into the person that God has always intended them to be. It is amazing to see the light come on in someone's eyes as they begin to realize that their lives can make a difference and that their gifts and skills are important to the kingdom of God.

I have never really understood why people feel threatened by the gifts and skills of others. It seems to me that if you are a God gazer, you will want others not only to see the beauty and the wonder of God but also to experience the amazing reality of the life-giving, world-changing power of God flow through them and out to other people. A fear of being outshone can cause us to stop other people from shining. A fear of somehow being unnoticed or forgotten can cause us to try and force other people to stand in our shadow, but such attitudes show the smallness of our hearts. God doesn't treat us like that, so why should we treat others with such fear or anxiety. Perhaps the root of it all is a search for significance in all the wrong places and a belief that we need to be better at something than anyone else. Does it really matter if someone else is better than you are or I am at something? I think the most important thing is that we are the best that we can be.

The idea of having to be better than everyone else causes us to have a threatened and fearful outlook. We will always wonder who is coming up behind us and what we have to do to stay ahead of them. I wouldn't like to live like that. I'd much rather my attitude be one that releases, encourages, and inspires other people to shine. I really believe that a local church pastor needs to have an approach to other people in his or her church family that is always looking for the possibilities in them. Good pastors – in fact, good Christians and good leaders – are always looking for ways of enabling people to shine.

The kingdom is extended when we allow people to fulfil their potential.

You could describe this approach as one that enables people to flourish. I like that idea. What can I do to help other people to flourish? How can I bring the best out in others? How can I make room for them to thrive? Imagine what you could achieve with your life if you chose to remember that the greatest thing you could leave was a legacy that helped other people to grow. Imagine the power of believing that the ceiling of your achievements would be nothing more than the floor of the generation that would follow you.

Wow.

When we are God gazers, we choose not to compare ourselves to other people. Instead, we live in the light of God's love for us and we bask in his grace and mercy. By doing so, we are freed to release and encourage others. We understand that the gospel is not ours to keep, to change, or to manipulate. Instead we know that the gospel is like a baton that has been entrusted to us for a while and which we must pass on to others *faithfully* and *intact*. That's important to remember because we are not free to change the message of the good news. In releasing and raising others up, we must remain true to the message of the cross and the reality that Christ came to bear our sin, to pay the penalty of our wrongs, and to carry the wrath of God. As he did so, God counted us as righteous and credited us with the standing that Christ had, at the same time placing the penalty of our sin upon Christ (2 Corinthians 5:21).

This gospel has been under attack in almost every generation since the birth of the church. There have always been those who have tried to make it into something else.

We must resist such attempts, not just for our own sake but also for the sake of those who come after us. The gospel is the only thing that can truly change the world, and it is the only thing that can truly change a human heart. We must never try to change it or water it down or make it more palatable. Instead we must understand that we have been entrusted with this great treasure and we must pass it on to others with the same strong expectations as those with which Paul passed it on to the young pastor, Timothy (2 Timothy 4:2–5).

But what has all of this got to do with releasing others? Well, we release others in every way that we can. We encourage them to try new things, to engage in new ways, to push into territory that we have never dreamed of. We hold up their arms and encourage them to have a go, but we never compromise on the centrality of the Lord Jesus Christ, and we guard against *any* and *every* attempt to change the fundamental nature of the gospel and the message of the cross. We release others to be true to their own calling and their own purposes, but we do so knowing that this will never demand a contradiction of the truth of the gospel or the centrality of the cross. People flourish most when they know who they are *in Christ* and when they are released *in Christ* to become all that he has made them to be.

I have seen so many church leaders handle badly the issue of releasing and encouraging others. It is a tragedy. Some hold on to their positions and their titles and their pulpits for far too long. They see the local church they lead as their property, and they are fearful of anyone else leading it forward. As a result, they become ever more suspicious and anxious. They find it incredibly difficult to praise or affirm anyone else for fear of feeling themselves to be less affirmed. Attitudes like this lead to deep heartbreak in the lives of those who long to be released, and deep frustrations in the congregations who want to see the kingdom of God grow and flourish.

Transitions in churches, business, and ministries are always difficult, but not impossible. If you adopt the basic principle of always trying to work yourself out of a job, I guarantee that there will always be something for you to do!

One of the key ways in which we can be Life givers is by enabling people to flourish. We can nurture, affirm, encourage, and release others to fulfil the calling of God in their lives. If we can learn the art of doing that, we will strengthen the witness of the kingdom of God, we will undermine the terrible cult of "personality" that has blighted much of Western Christianity, and we will build a wonderful platform for those who come after us to go further than we have ever gone. That sounds like a winning outcome all round to me.

I can think of no better example of a releaser in the Bible than the remarkable man, Barnabas, so I would like to examine his life and see what he can teach us about being a Life giver who releases others to be the best that they can be.

Barnabas – the forgotten hero

Barnabas is mentioned twenty-eight times in the New Testament. The remarkable thing is that his name is mentioned twenty-three times in the book of Acts. Of those occurrences, he is mentioned once in chapter 4, once in chapter 9, three times in chapter 11, once in chapter 12, six times in chapter 13, three times in chapter 14, and eight times in chapter 15. He is also mentioned once in the letters to the Corinthians, three times in the letter to the Galatians, and once in the letter to the Colossians. I am not listing them all to bore you but rather to show you that he was an important figure in the early church. In many ways he is a forgotten hero. I know that he is not mentioned as many times as John (132 times), or Peter (151 times), or Paul (160 times), but Barnabas is nevertheless a very important and often overlooked figure in the story of the fledgling church. I very much doubt whether Paul would have fulfilled a significant ministry at all if it had not been for the wisdom and the encouragement and the persistence of Barnabas, and I know that John Mark would have been consigned to the rubbish dump of failure had it not been for Barnabas.

Barnabas teaches us a great deal about what it means to release and encourage others. His life is a picture of investing in others, giving them a chance, and helping them to flourish. Granted, he was not perfect (the mentions of him in Galatians 2 are because he was drawn into the controversy that also affected Peter when there was an attempt to draw the early church back into the Jewish faith), but he was a remarkable man who left an incredible legacy, and he has much to teach us about being releasers.

There are four aspects of Barnabas' life and ministry that I want to highlight.

The lesson of encouragement

The first mention of Barnabas is at the end of Acts 4:

> There was a Levite, a native of Cyprus, Joseph, to
> whom the apostles gave the name Barnabas (which
> means "son of encouragement"). He sold a field
> that belonged to him, then brought the money, and
> laid it at the apostles' feet.

Acts 4:36–37

Barnabas was the name given to him because he was such
an encourager. His real name was Joseph. He was given
the name because of his action in selling a field that he
owned and giving the proceeds to the apostles to distribute
among the needs of the early church. Immediately we see
a trait of this man that will appear again and again. He
used his resources to encourage others. Where there was a
need and he could do something about it, he did so.

We must never underestimate the power of
encouragement in the life of another human being.
Barnabas understood this. As we will see in his dealings
with Paul, with John Mark, and with the leaders of the
church in Jerusalem, Barnabas sought to build others up,
to support them, to help them. If we want to be releasers,
we need to be encouragers. We will seek to build others up
in their faith and we will come alongside them.

The lesson of confidence in his own gifts and calling

The church in Antioch commissioned Barnabas, at the
command of the Holy Spirit, to travel throughout the
region and proclaim Jesus:

> Now in the church in Antioch there were prophets
> and teachers: Barnabas, Simeon who was called
> Niger, Lucius of Cyrene, Manean a member of
> the court of Herod the ruler, and Saul. While they
> were worshipping the Lord and fasting, the Holy
> Spirit said, "Set apart for me Barnabas and Saul for
> the work to which I have called them." Then after
> fasting and praying they laid their hands on them
> and sent them off.

Acts 13:1–3

Not only was Barnabas an encourager; he was also confident and gifted. The Lord's hand was clearly upon him to such an extent that he and Paul were pinpointed by the Holy Spirit to be commissioned for the work of spreading the gospel and planting churches. This is a remarkable incident in the life of the early church, not least because Barnabas had been the one who had encouraged Paul and supported and affirmed him.

To release others, we need to be confident in the hand of God upon our own lives. It is only when we think that the promotion or the releasing of someone else might threaten or undermine us that we become fearful. Barnabas had no such anxieties. In fact, he almost entirely disappears from the latter part of the story of the early church in the book of Acts as the apostle Paul takes on a more central role, but there is no evidence to suggest that this was an issue for Barnabas at all.

This leads us to the third lesson that Barnabas teaches us about releasing others.

The lesson of not needing to be the centre of attention

When Paul arrived in Jerusalem in Acts 9, most of the other apostles were suspicious of him, but Barnabas is not:

> When [Paul] had come to Jerusalem, he attempted to join the disciples; and they were all afraid of him, for they did not believe that he was a disciple. But Barnabas took him, brought him to the apostles, and described for them how on the road he had seen the Lord, who had spoken to him, and how in Damascus he had spoken boldly in the name of Jesus.
>
> **Acts 9:26–27**

Later, the church was scattered and some of the believers ended up in Antioch. Something of a move of the Holy Spirit took place and the Jerusalem church needed to send someone to Antioch to support and encourage the believers there. They sent Barnabas. What is remarkable is what Barnabas did when he arrived in Antioch and saw what was happening:

> When [Barnabas] came and saw the grace of God, he rejoiced, and he exhorted them all to remain faithful to the Lord with steadfast devotion; for he was a good man, full of the Holy Spirit and of faith. And a great many people were brought to the Lord. Then Barnabas went to Tarsus to look for Saul, and when he had found him, he brought him to Antioch. So it was that for an entire year they associated with the church and taught a great many people, and it was in Antioch that the disciples were first called "Christians".
>
> **Acts 11:23–26**

Here we see Barnabas sent by the Jerusalem church to encourage and support what the Lord was doing in Antioch. The passage tells us much about the calibre and strength of Barnabas' own ministry and influence. It also tells us that as he saw what was happening in Antioch he recognized that he needed the help and support of someone else, and he knew exactly who that was. Barnabas travelled to Tarsus and brought Paul back to Antioch, and they embarked on a joint ministry of teaching and encouragement. Barnabas was not concerned about his own reputation; he was not worried about bringing someone else into the leadership of the church in Antioch. He was not afraid to step to one side to let someone else serve and exercise their ministry.

Life givers release others to fulfil their God-given potential. Like Barnabas, they are not afraid to move sideways, or indeed to move out of the way, when it is right to do so. If we are to release others, we must learn the lesson that it is not about us, but about what is best for the kingdom of God. If we are to release others, we must embrace the fact that we do not need to be the centre of attention. God's purposes are always more important than our preferences. If God has someone who is able to serve in a situation with more effectiveness than we are, we should be willing and open to moving so that the kingdom of God can be advanced and others can be enabled and released.

The lesson of giving people a chance

Not only did Barnabas give Paul a chance, as we see in Acts 11, but he also gave John Mark (Barnabas' nephew) a chance. After the Council of Jerusalem, recorded in Acts 15, Paul suggested to Barnabas that the two of them should return to the cities where they had previously ministered (note that Paul is now leading Barnabas and not the other way round). Barnabas wanted to take John Mark with them but Paul did not want to take him because John Mark had left them on a previous missionary journey. Barnabas and Paul argued strongly over the issue and actually went in separate directions:

> The disagreement became so sharp that they parted company; Barnabas took Mark with him and sailed away to Cyprus. But Paul chose Silas and set out, the believers commending him to the grace of the Lord. He went through Syria and Cilicia, strengthening the churches.
>
> **Acts 15:39–41**

Paul was not willing to give John Mark a chance, but Barnabas was. Just as he had given Paul himself a chance when the believers in Jerusalem were suspicious of him, so Barnabas was not willing to write John Mark off. As it turned out, Paul acknowledged some years later that John Mark should not have been written off. Towards the end of his life Paul wrote to Timothy and asked him to send John Mark because John Mark was "useful" to Paul's ministry (2 Timothy 4:11). Barnabas was not willing to give up on the young John Mark because of one mistake.

Barnabas exits the story of the book of Acts as unnoticeably as he enters it. Yet even in this I think we can hear echoes of the teaching of the Lord Jesus, who said that those who want to be great should be servants (Matthew 20:26). We never really hear from Barnabas again. He was right to believe in Paul, though, and he was right to believe in John Mark.

Barnabas was a releaser. He welcomed Gentile churches when such a move was difficult and perhaps even dangerous for a Jew. He moved to new places and served in new ways when God called him to because his life was reorientated around the purposes of God after his conversion.

If I think back over my life and examine the traits of the people who have released me or encouraged me or helped me grow, they are all people remarkably like Barnabas. They believed in me, they supported me, they strengthened my soul, and they encouraged me to continue in the faith, just like Barnabas (Acts 14:22).

Life givers who want to release others are willing both to take a risk and to give people a chance. They do not write someone off because of one mistake but instead they believe in them, support them, and give them the opportunity to learn from their mistake. I am so grateful for the many, many times that someone has been willing to give me another chance. Looking back over my life and ministry I can think of many people who were willing to give me a chance: John Glass in the Elim Pentecostal Church; Joel Edwards at the Evangelical Alliance; Steve Chalke in Faithworks; Brian Baldwin and the Countess of Huntingdon Connexion; David Coffey and the Baptist Union; the leadership of Gold Hill; the leadership team of Spring Harvest; Tony Collins and the editorial team at Lion Hudson; my friend Lyndon Bowring. The list goes on and on and on. These people are all releasers, and I do not know where I would be without them. Releasers see something in someone else and they are willing to take a risk, to step out in trust, and to give someone the opportunity to shine, to make a difference.

What a glorious trait to develop – to see someone and give him or her a chance to shine. You will let them pass you by and excel beyond what you have achieved. Releasers do that. They take chances; they believe in people. They let others try.

I wonder what my nickname would be if my friends gave me one? Would it be "Encourager"? Would it be "Releaser"? What about you? What would your nickname be if your friends had to give you one?

Barnabas teaches us many more lessons. He shows us that we can support ourselves when the need arises (1 Corinthians 9:6). He shows us that the long term is more important than the immediate (Colossians 4:10). He shows us the power of forgiveness, and that friendships and relationships are worth investing in and protecting: his relationship with Paul is not permanently fractured. These attributes as well as the four that I have focused in on show us what it means to be a releaser.

We, too, can be generous encouragers. We, too, can be confident enough in our own gifts and calling not to be threatened by others. We, too, can decide not to be the centre of attention. We, too, can give people a chance and take risks.

Would other people describe us as releasers?

> I want to be a Life giver!
> A "you can do it" releaser,
> a "have a go" preacher,
> a "you were born to do this" pastor.

As I reread this stanza of *God Gazer* I was struck by how aptly it describes people like Barnabas. It is my deep hope that these words describe my own attitude to ministry and to others. Ultimately, however, we are not the measure of our own ability to release and to encourage others. Those to whom we minister and those with whom we minister must make that judgment because we are ill-placed and ill-equipped to make the judgment fairly and honestly. What we can do is make sure that we never exclude someone because of fear.

So many people have lost the gift of aspiration because they have been denied the opportunity to try. I wonder how we could start a virus of possibility in our churches, our ministries, our families, our communities, and our societies. Are there ways in which we can deliberately and intentionally sow the possibility of something fresh and new into the lives of others?

I think there are many ways in which we can do this. We can affirm people when they get something right. We can be thankful. We can listen carefully and prayerfully to the stories of other people's lives. We can take an interest in them. We can pray for them. We can mentor them. We can invest in them over a cup of coffee. We can tell them the truth. We can help them plot their futures and explore their destinies. We can create spaces and places for people to try new things, to dream new dreams, and to attempt new ventures. We can have an attitude to failure that refuses to see it as fatal and instead sees it as an opportunity to learn and grow. In our churches we can develop cultures of possibility and entrepreneurship and hope. We can give room and space for new ideas. If we are preachers, we can preach hopefully; we can point out the stories of those in the Bible who attempted great things for God. We can invite those who are breaking new ground to come and share in the lives of our communities of faith. We can listen to new ideas; we can be open to learning new things and seeing situations through someone else's eyes. We can listen to the frustrations of those who feel that things need to change. We can be humble enough to acknowledge that there might be something to learn from someone else. We can keep an open mind.

Being a releaser doesn't begin somewhere else in our churches: it begins with you and me. It begins in us.

If we are ever to be releasers, we ourselves must experience release. How does that happen? It happens when we have a fresh vision of who God is and what he has for our lives, and so we return to the basic and unmoveable premise of this book: God gazers are Life givers because they are God gazers.

Why not use the next stanza of *God Gazer* as a prayer? Ask God to instil in you a deep longing for those around you to excel, to shine, to flourish, and then find a way of deliberately encouraging them and intentionally creating an opportunity for them to try. Even if they make a mistake, you can make sure that mistake is not fatal. You can be there to applaud them if they succeed and to pick them up if they fall and to celebrate their courage, their passion, and their vision no matter what happens.

> I want to be a Life giver!
> Seeing rivers flow, not die,
> seeing others rise and fly,
> helping friends reach for the stars
> even if they sometimes miss,
> at least they can say they tried.

Jesus was a Life giver. He took risks. Whether that was with the woman at the well with whom he had a conversation, breaking every social taboo in the book, or whether it was having dinner with the outcasts and the hated, such as Zacchaeus or Mary Magdalene. He refused to be bound by other people's expectations of him. He didn't care what self-righteous people thought of him. He wasn't interested in maintaining the status quo. He wanted those who had been beaten down by the religious authorities to know that he had come to set them free.

He was a releaser. He was a Life giver. He released people from old restrictions. He spoke with women and he let them sit at his feet like a rabbi's student. He welcomed the outcasts. He spent time with the unclean. He touched lepers. He raised the dead. He called fishermen and ignored the well-educated. He was never interested in meeting Herod, but he was determined to meet that woman at the well. He went out of his way to do so. That tells us something about his attitude, doesn't it? He announced his releasing ministry when he walked into the synagogue in Nazareth and read from the scroll of Isaiah. You will never see a more Life-giving, releasing intention than that. And his manifesto is our manifesto because the purpose of his ministry is the purpose of our lives:

> He unrolled the scroll and found the place where it was written:
> "The Spirit of the Lord is upon me,
> because he has anointed me
> to bring good news to the poor.
> He has sent me to proclaim release to the captives
> and recovery of sight to the blind,
> to let the oppressed go free,
> to proclaim the year of the Lord's favour."
>
> And he rolled up the scroll, gave it back to the attendant, and sat down. The eyes of all in the synagogue were fixed on him. Then he began to say to them, "Today this scripture has been fulfilled in your hearing."

Luke 4:17–21

No matter where you look, you will never find more releasing, life-giving, hope-inducing words than these. This is the Releaser's declaration of intent. This is the Life-giving power of the gospel given to us and placed within us. We, too, have this commission.

Best get on with it.

CHAPTER ELEVEN

A Drainpipe Without Blockages

I want to be a Life giver!
A drainpipe without blockages,
a circuit without stoppages,
a connector without breakages.

I hate death because I was made for life.

Death and destruction and disease are intruders in the world. God has permitted them, and he even uses the responses of his people to them to bring further glory to his name, but make no mistake about it: we were not made to die; we were made to live. It is in our DNA. It is part of our humanity that we want to live. From the first determined cry of a baby to the last gasp before we leave this world, we fight for life. We do so because we were made for life. God is a God of life. He is a God who brings life, who upholds life, who sustains life. He is the God who draws us through the valley of the shadow of death and into the land of the living (Psalm 118:17).

Despite the fact that we were made for life, we find ourselves facing death. We live in a world where death is commonplace, where it is part of the order of things. Of course we know that this is the case because sin has impacted the whole of the world (Romans 8). Sin has affected our humanity and left us fallen (Genesis 3), and sin has left us with a natural propensity to do our own thing and to ignore God's purposes and plans because we each choose to do our own thing and live our own way rather than God's way (Romans 3).

However, when we become Christians, we are given a new desire and a new nature (2 Corinthians 5). We are no longer simply controlled by the old way of thinking and the old way of living (Romans 6–7). We now have the ability to live differently. We do not have to be controlled by our old worldview and mindset (Galatians 5). We have a choice! We can choose life (Deuteronomy 28). We can choose to bring life to others. We can choose to be a source of hope and life in our family, our community, and our society. When we go to work, God comes with us. When we go to school or college or university, God comes with us. We are not only people who have come to know him whom to know is life eternal (John 17:3); we are also carriers of that life wherever we go and whatever we do. We carry the life of God in us, we carry the presence of God with us, and we are ambassadors for the kingdom of God in every single situation that we face and no matter where we are. We not only understand that Jesus is the light of the world (John 8:12); we ourselves are also carriers of that light (Matthew 5:14–16).

It is natural, therefore, that we want to ensure that any *blockage* to the life of God flowing through us is dealt with. We do not want anything to get in the way of God moving through us and touching the lives of those around us. How do we become a "drainpipe without blockages, a circuit without stoppages, a connector without breakages"?

Sin

The obvious blockage in our lives is sin. There are a number of words that are used in the New Testament which are translated "sin". One group of these words includes *hamartia*, *hamartema*, and *hamartano*.

The most common of the words used is *hamartia* and it is most often translated as "sin" or "sins". The word literally means "missing the mark", but the New Testament idea of sin also conveys the idea of something that has been warped or broken within us. In the New Testament, sin is seen as an element or a principle within human beings (Romans 5:12, 20; 6:1–2). It is also seen as a power or a force which controls and dominates those who are not Christians and distorts the way they view themselves, God, and the world (John 8:34; Romans 3:9; 5:21; 6:6, 17, 20; 8:2). In this sense sin is something that enslaves and ensnares those who commit it (John 8:34). Thirdly, sin is an expression of rebellion and lawlessness towards God (1 John 3:4). Fourthly, to be "in sin" is to be in a state of spiritual death (Ephesians 2:1, 5), into which all humans are born and from which we can only be delivered by being born again by God's Spirit (John 3:3–6). Fifthly, sin is anything in our character and conduct that does not fit with God's character and heart (1 John 5:17). Sin is, sixthly, an act or something that we do or commit (Matthew 12:31; Acts 7:60; James 1:15a; 2:9; 4:17; 5:15, 20).

The second word in this group is *hamartema*, which means "an act of disobedience to the law of God" and is used several times in the New Testament (Mark 3:28; Romans 3:25; 1 Corinthians 6:18).

The third word in this group is the word *hamartano*, and it means "to act contrary to the will and the law of God". It is used to describe the rebellion of angels against God (2 Peter 2:4) and human actions against God (Luke 15:18, 21; John 5:14; 8:11; Romans 3:23; 5:12, 14, 16; 1 John 2:1 (twice); 3:6 (twice), 8, 9; 5:16 (twice)). It is used to describe one human's actions against another human being (Matthew 18:15; Luke 17:3-4; 1 Corinthians 8:12). It is also used to describe some of the ways in which we treat our own bodies, particularly with regard to sexual activity (1 Corinthians 6:18).

In addition to the *hamartia* word group for sin, there are four others that are used in the Bible. The Greek word group *parabasis* is used to convey the idea of stepping across a forbidden line intentionally and indicates a willful and deliberate decision to act against what we know to be true and right. The Greek word group *paratoma* is used to convey the idea that sin is slipping across a perceived boundary unintentionally. The Greek word group *anomia* is used to describe sin as an act of lawlessness and an assertion of independence and refusal to be accountable. Lastly, the Greek word group *opheilema* is used to convey the sense of sin as an indebtedness or a trespass or an outstanding charge. These concepts and ideas, combined with the intrinsic meaning of the *hamartia* word group as missing the mark provide a challenging outline of the Bible's teaching on sin and what it is. Whether it be missing the target, willfully or involuntarily crossing a line of right thinking, attitudes or behaviour, a refusal to be accountable or an outstanding charge debt or obligation, the Bible presents sin as a serious issue for the lives of men and women. It is not one that we can ignore. It is the major blockage in our lives when it comes to our relationship with God, with other people and out understanding of ourselves.

I realise that the last few paragraphs are densely packed with Bible references and Greek words, but it is important that we acknowledge the depth of information contained in the Bible when it comes to sin. The "sin issue" is such an important one that we cannot and should not rush past it. The descriptions of sin show us that this issue affects every single human being and that we cannot avoid it.

Now I know that there are many people in the Christian Church today who want to do away with the idea of sin. They tell us that we should not be worried about it because sin does not affect the life of the Christian. They look at passages like Paul's description of his struggle with sin in Romans 6 and 7 and they say that he was clearly describing his life *before* he was Christian. As far back as John Wesley in the seventeenth century, Christians were talking about the notion that we can live completely free from sin. Further back than that we have Pelagius (354–420), who argued that we were not born in sin and that the notion of original sin should be rejected. The difficulty with such notions is that they do not stack up. They do not stack up against the wealth of New Testament evidence about sin, and they do not stack up against the reality of human experience.

Sin blocks our relationship with God. It causes pride, fear, resentment, and a wealth of other things. It either makes us feel that we are useless and terrible or it makes us feel that we are all powerful and invincible. There are many Christians who think that they have completely overcome sin, and thus fall into the sin of pride and arrogance and self-reliance. There are equally as many who think that they are useless and hopeless and filthy because they have been taught to be so sin-conscious that they have no awareness of grace. However it assaults us, the devil wants us to be preoccupied with sin. It is the cause of every problem in our lives and in our relationships with God and with each other. It is the issue that makes us feel so useless or so arrogant.

Life givers have to deal with the sin issue. We have to address it properly so that we can be people who have no blockages in our lives. We must not be dominated or controlled by it, but we must not ignore it either. If you are reading these words and think that you are hopelessly caught in sin or that you will never get over this issue, then take hope and read on!

Jesus Christ dealt with sin on the cross

The Bible tells us the most remarkable thing about sin. It tells us that Jesus Christ dealt with all sin on the cross. I know that sounds incredible, but it is true. Let me show you just two Scriptures that help us to see this:

> The next day [John the Baptist] saw Jesus coming
> toward him and declared, "Here is the Lamb of
> God who takes away the sin of the whole world!"
>
> **John 1:29**

> My little children, I am writing these things to you
> so that you may not sin. But if anyone does sin, we
> have an advocate with the Father, Jesus Christ the

righteous; and he is the atoning sacrifice for our
sins, and not for ours only but also for the sins of
the world.

1 John 2:1–2

Now these two portions of the Bible are quite remarkable.
Read them again, slowly. They do not say that Jesus dealt
with *your* sin. They do not say that Jesus dealt with the sin
of the church only. They say much more than that. They tell
us that Jesus Christ dealt with the *sins of the whole world*.
Do you see that? Do you see how all encompassing that
is? Do you see how important that is? Allow it to sink in.
Jesus has dealt with every single aspect of sin.

Go back and read the densely packed Bible references
at the beginning of this chapter again. Think about every
single barrier, every single blockage, and every single
stoppage. Then imagine that you take a large red pen and
you put a line through every single one, because Jesus has
dealt with them all. This is the most astounding claim I
have ever heard, and yet it is true. From the first sin that
was ever committed to the last one that lies ahead of us in
time and history, Jesus has dealt with them all. From the
issue of our fallen nature to the issue of our hearts that are
bent in upon themselves, Jesus has dealt with them all.

The people of the Old Testament and the people of
the New Testament are all liberated from the power and
the influence of sin by the fact that Jesus has dealt with it
all. There was not one way of being rescued from sin for
the Jews of the Old Testament and another way of being
rescued from sin for those who lived after the death of
Jesus. That is not at all what the Bible teaches. Instead, the
Bible teaches that Jesus is the Lamb who was slain *for the*

sins of the whole world, and that he is the Lamb who was slain before the foundation of the world (Revelation 13:8). Listen to the remarkable way in which Peter describes this truth:

> You know that you were ransomed from the
> futile ways inherited from your ancestors, not
> with perishable things like silver or gold, but with
> the precious blood of Christ, like that of a lamb
> without defect or blemish. He was destined before
> the foundation of the world, but was revealed at
> the end of the ages for your sake. Through him you
> have come to trust in God, who raised him from
> the dead and gave him glory, so that your faith and
> hope are set on God.

1 Peter 1:18–21

It is not my intention in this little book to go into the deep and staggering beauty of how Christ paid for our sin upon the cross: that is for another time. What I must say, however, is that as Jesus died, he was taking the punishment that we deserved so that we might be declared righteous and justified by God (Romans 3:21–31). It was the blood of Jesus that bought our redemption. His sacrifice upon the cross satisfied the demands of a righteous and holy God. Jesus defeated sin on the cross. His blood was shed for us. It is his blood that has purchased our freedom and our liberty. His death on the cross means that all sin has been dealt with. He has done it! He has paid the price! He has borne our sin!

We appropriate what Jesus has done for us through faith

"What, then, are the blockages that we must deal with, Malcolm, if we are to be free from sin and its power?" you might now be asking. "If Jesus dealt with sin on the cross, then you must be saying that all people are forgiven and all people are now saved." No, that is not what I am saying.

There is an old phrase in the Christian church that we must remember: it is that the cross of Christ is *sufficient* for all but *efficient* in those who believe. Read that again, slowly. The cross of Christ is *sufficient* for all but *efficient* in those who believe. That means that your sin will not take you to a lost eternity and separation from God because Christ has dealt with your sin. What will take you to a place of separation from God is whether or not you believe the amazing message of the gospel to be true.

Be careful to hear what I am saying. It is not your faith that will save you. It is not your faith that deals with the blockages, the stoppages, and the breakages. That is not what I have said. It is the death of Jesus and the death of Jesus alone that saves you. If you believe this, if you have faith in this startling truth, then you are saved. If you do not believe it, then you are not saved. If you believe it, then every blockage is removed. If you do not, then no amount of good works or nice things or churchgoing or Bible reading or praying or praising or giving to the poor will save you. Listen to the words of Jesus himself:

> For God so loved the world that he gave his only Son, so that everyone who believes in him may not perish but may have eternal life.

> Indeed, God did not send the Son into the world
> to condemn the world, but in order that the world
> might be saved through him. Those who believe
> in him are not condemned; but those who do not
> believe are condemned already, because they have
> not believed in the name of the only Son of God.

John 3:16–18

If we believe that Jesus died for us, that through his death we have been declared legally righteous, then every blockage is removed.

This is an amazing reality, isn't it? Nothing to earn and nothing to prove. Nothing in us that is worthy of such love and grace, yet this total forgiveness and liberation is available to us. All we need to do is accept it in faith and believe it.

And it gets better. Although we are not perfect, we still sin and still fall and still make mistakes (1 John makes this abundantly clear), when we accept what Jesus has done on the cross for us, we are not only forgiven; we are also declared righteous (Romans 3). The term that is translated as "justified" in Romans 3:20 (see also Romans 5:1–11) in the NRSV can also be translated as "declared righteous". The phrase is actually an accounting term. It means that something is credited to our account. This is a divine exchange that goes beyond our wildest dreams and hopes. As Jesus dies for us, God takes his purity and righteousness and places it over our sin, and he takes our sin and places it on Jesus. We are accounted righteous and Jesus bears our sin. We are not made perfect through the death of Jesus; we are declared righteous, and we are justified. We are forgiven and we are released! Hallelujah!

The apostle Paul goes on to explain that the death and the resurrection of Jesus not only secure our forgiveness and our justification; they also guarantee our sanctification and our glorification (Romans 8).

What an astounding salvation! And it is all given to us through faith, which is a gracious gift also given to us by God and not something that we have whipped up or created for ourselves (Ephesians 2). So you see, our blockages and stoppages and breakages have been dealt with, but do we believe this astounding good news to be true?

Does this mean that I need not be conscious of my sin at all?

The next fundamental question that I would be asking if I were you is where this leaves the whole question of how I deal with the sins that I commit now. Do I need to confess these sins now or not? Am I not still a sinner? These are very interesting, and very important, questions.

Let me deal with the question of confession first. The apostle John makes it very clear in his first general epistle that we are still impacted by sin because we still commit sin. He also says that if we confess our sins, God is faithful and just and will forgive our sins and cleanse us from all unrighteousness (1 John 1:7–9).

This is important to understand because there is a dangerous teaching doing the rounds in the church today, called the teaching of hyper-grace. It tells you that you do not need to worry about your sin, because it has all been dealt with. It tells you that what John means when he talks about confession is that we should simply confess who we are in Christ now and forget about what we used to be.

As with many errors in the church, there is an element of truth in this teaching, but there is also a great deal of error. It is true that many Christians have been taught to have a heavy sin consciousness that needs to be rebalanced, and it is true that we must not become obsessed with sin. The error is to suggest that this means we must pretend we do not sin. That is a sin in itself, according to John's epistle! If we say that we are without sin, John says, we are deceiving ourselves and, worse still, we make God himself a liar and the truth is not in us (1 John 1:8–10).

What, then, is the answer? John's argument is not linear; it is cylindrical. He was writing to a group of people who had been duped into two equally wrong positions. One was that they were free from sin and could do what they liked; the other was that they were trapped by sin and there was no way out. His answer is the answer to our question. He tells his listeners that they must remember that even though they continue to sin, they have a powerful advocate with the Father in Jesus Christ who has paid the penalty for their sin and who has secured their forgiveness. He tells them that they do not need to pretend to be perfect because they are clearly still people who sin, but he also tells them that they are to constantly and continually rest in what Jesus has done for them. In humility they confess that they sin, but with hope and assurance they live in the power of Christ's mercy and forgiveness secured for them in the cross.

This is exactly what we must learn to do. We are no longer simply sinners. We may be people who sin. We may be people who make mistakes, but we are now saints who sin. We run to the Father, who has secured our forgiveness through his Son. We stand in boldness and in confidence in the very presence of God because our sin has been dealt with. There are no blockages. Every blockage, every stoppage, every breakage was dealt with when Jesus died, and we can now have confidence in our new identity in Christ. We will never be separated from him. We will never be cast away from him. We are loved. We are forgiven and we are accepted in Christ! Our communion will not be broken.

The extent to which we enjoy this remarkable and Life-giving reality is determined by the extent to which we believe it.

Do you believe it?

It almost sounds too good to be true, doesn't it?

But it is true. It is the truest thing you will ever hear, and it is the most Life-giving and transforming theological reality you will ever hear. Nothing, absolutely nothing, can separate us from the love of God in Christ Jesus (Romans 8).

Do you believe it?

The impact of believing that we are forgiven

> I want to be a Life giver!
> Generous in spirit and in heart,
> letting the forgotten make a start
> at being Life givers, too.

When we understand the amazing grace that has been shown to us, it becomes our heart's desire to see other people make this discovery, too. The impact of believing in what Jesus has done for us on the cross is that it releases us from any sense of self-righteousness. There is nothing we have done that can ever mean we deserve the grace and the mercy of God. When we realize that, we become much more humble in our understanding of ourselves and of other people. We realize that we are all broken people. We recognize that the only thing that separates us from those who do not know Christ is the fact that we have come to see and to believe in what he has done for us, and they have not.

This realization destroys any sense of condescension in us and helps us to appreciate that being a Christian does not make us better than anyone. Instead, we realize that being a Christian means that we want to show the same generosity and kindness to others as Christ has shown to us. We want those around us to see and experience the incredible mercy and love and forgiveness of God, too. We understand that we are one of many who have come to experience the love of God, and we want to let others in on the secret. Christians cannot help but share the incredible, astounding, breathtaking love that God has for people.

When you discover just how much God has done for you, the inevitable consequence is that you want others to know how much God has done for them, too. Not only that, but you also want people to reach their full potential in Christ. You want to believe the best of them, see the best in them, and release the best in them.

In Luke 7 a woman with a sinful past washed Jesus' feet with her tears and wiped them with her hair. The event took place in the house of a Pharisee who was judgmental and cold towards the woman and critical of Jesus for letting her wash his feet. Jesus challenged the Pharisee and told him that the woman loved much because she had been forgiven much. That captures the heart of what happens in the lives of God gazers. We realize that we have been forgiven *everything*, and as a result we want other people to experience the forgiveness of God and encounter the acceptance and the beauty and the hope that comes from a relationship with God. Our whole lives become centred around Jesus and what he has done for us. We recognize that we are completely and utterly reliant upon him for life. Life givers realize that our lives are no longer about us; they are about him. We want our actions, our thoughts, our hopes, our dreams, and everything about us to point to him.

Life givers know that they cannot bring life to anyone. Life givers know that there is only one hero in the story of their lives, and his name is Jesus. They know that the world has only one hero because they know that the world has only one Saviour, and his name is Jesus. Life givers know that their blood was not shed to save anyone, but Jesus' blood can set people free. Life givers know that there is no reason for people to remain trapped in misery and sin because Jesus has paid the price. He has opened the prison doors. He has borne the cost. Life givers point to the Source of life. They want their lives to reflect his life and they want everyone around them to see and experience this amazing source of life, too. Life givers know that the person whom the Son sets free is free indeed (John 8:36), and they know that the shallow existence that the devil has tricked people into living is nothing compared to the abundant life that Jesus promises (John 10:10).

Oh, I want to be a Life giver! I want my whole family to know that this is true. I weep for them because I know that many of them still do not see it. They think I am mad. They think I am too religious. They don't understand that I am not religious at all. They don't see that I am not good at all. I want them all – my brothers and my sister and their partners and my nephews and my nieces – to see the amazing love and grace and hope that is available to them through the Source. I want everyone in my village to see it. I want them to experience the Life-giving power of Jesus!

I want our village to be rebuilt on this hope. I want every young person in our schools to know that this is true. I want our county to see it. I want our nation to see that the only thing that can bring them Life, real Life, is the power of what Jesus has done for them.

Isn't that your longing? Don't you burst with longing to see your community changed? Can't you feel your heart beat like a drum within your chest at such a thought? Doesn't it drive you to your knees in longing and in worship and in prayer?

Don't you want the world to see him, to know him, to love him, and to experience the reality that he loves them?

> I want to be a Life giver
> Connected to the Source
> and pointing to the Son.
> Standing in the shadow of the Light,
> celebrating him.
>
> I want to be a Life giver
> because I am a God gazer.
> Not because it's about me
> but because it's about him.
> Because life can't spring
> from any other "thing".

SECTION THREE

"World Changers"

*Then I saw a new heaven and a new earth; for the
first heaven and the first earth had passed away, and
the sea was no more. And I saw the holy city, the new
Jerusalem, coming down out of heaven from God,
prepared as a bride adorned for her husband. And I
heard a loud voice from the throne saying,*

*"See, the home of God is among mortals.
He will dwell with them;
they will be his peoples,
and God himself will be with them;
he will wipe every tear from their eyes.
Death will be no more;
mourning and crying and pain will be no more,
for the first things have passed away."*

Revelation 21:1–4

*The whole difference between construction and
creation is exactly this; that a thing constructed
can only be loved after it is constructed but a thing
created is loved before it exists.*

G. K. Chesterton[13]

13 G. K. Chesterton, *Collected Works, Volume XV: Chesterton on Dickens*, San
Francisco: Ignatius Press, 1989, p.246.

CHAPTER TWELVE

Not Just a Furniture Re-Arranger

I want to be a World changer
not just a furniture rearranger
or an "it could be better" whinger
or a "have the leftovers" stinger.

F ar too many Christians are either managing decline in their lives or are seeking to protect and to guard the status quo. We do this because we have turned the great and glorious message of the Life-giving God into a very advanced system of sin management. We have missed the beauty of the painting and have instead highlighted the high calibre of the picture frame or the canvas. What a tragedy.

Perhaps we do it because decline has become part of the experience of most churches and nations in the West for the last hundred years and we have therefore lowered our expectations because we have so often missed the target. Perhaps we have lowered our standards and our yearnings to avoid disappointment. Or maybe we have made the change in our approach to life because an understanding of Christianity that leads to moderate change and manageable reformation is much easier on our diaries, our wallets, and our consciences!

Our Christian lives have been neutered by a lack of expectation. We have allowed ourselves to think that we have achieved great things when we see one or two lives changed and our church buildings moderately full. Those of us who lead larger churches with longer histories often find ourselves in even more precarious and unbiblical positions. We have discovered that many in our congregations have lost the urgency of the gospel because they have come to understand their relationship with God as primarily about what he can do for them and how they can live a contented and fulfilled life in his service. The element of changing the world has been hidden by the comforts of life.

God, on the other hand, has a very different understanding of his purpose and plan for the world. He is changing the world, every last atom of it. He is not content with a little bit of niceness here and a little bit of religious sentimentality there. He is determined to bring the whole creation into a new place. He is not a divine furniture rearranger. He is a Creator and a Recreator. His plan and purpose is to bring all things, everything, every single thing, under the Lordship and the rule of Christ (Ephesians 1:10). He has made clear the central vehicle by which he intends to bring this about, and it is the church (Ephesians 2:10; 3:10). He has given the church gifts and he has led the church into new life so that the world might see who he is and may embrace his offer of life (Ephesians 4:10). We Christians are called to let God work through us in the everyday acts of kindness and generosity that he has given us to do (Ephesians 2:10; 5:10). We are called to win this battle on our knees, knowing that the devil wants to stop us, but knowing also that God has promised that we are on the winning side (Ephesians 6:10).

We are not called to simply maintain the status quo. We are not called to manage sin. We are not called to shuffle the current deck. We are called to see change. We are called to be the change that we want the world to see. We are called to be change bringers. We are called to be those who announce that God has broken into the world in the person and the work of Jesus Christ. Christians have the responsibility and the delight of announcing the kingdom of God and declaring the message of the gospel. We are not furniture rearrangers either. We are World changers. There is a vast difference between these two things. We are part of God's great purpose in the world, a purpose that is made clear to us through Paul's words to the Corinthians:

> So if anyone is in Christ, there is a new creation: everything old has passed away; see, everything has become new! All this is from God, who reconciled us to himself through Christ, and has given us the ministry of reconciliation; that is, in Christ God was reconciling the world to himself, not counting their trespasses against them, and entrusting the message of reconciliation to us. So we are ambassadors for Christ, since God is making his appeal through us; we entreat you on behalf of Christ, be reconciled to God. For our sake he made him to be sin who knew no sin, so that in him we might become the righteousness of God.
>
> **2 Corinthians 5:17–21**

There we have the great purposes of God clearly set out by the apostle Paul. Firstly, God is making all things new. God is *recreating*. He does this through the atoning death and resurrection of Jesus Christ. The gospel offers hope, forgiveness, and a fresh start by removing the barriers in our lives and by giving us the righteousness of Christ. The recreation is enabled by the divine exchange of Christ's righteousness and our sin. Secondly, God is drawing people back into relationship with himself and with one another. God is *reconciling*. This is achieved in the cross and the resurrection, too. We then, as Christians, are both new creations and part of the new creation. We are both reconciled and reconcilers. We are one of the central agencies through whom God is bringing hope to the world.

There are a few principles behind the idea of new creation that are important to understand.

New creation, not just reformation

It is extremely important to remember that God is not just taking the old bits of our lives and the world and attempting some kind of "fix-it-up" project. This is one of the fundamental mistakes that we make when we think about conversion and discipleship. God is not involved in repairing; he is involved in *new creation*. This is abundantly clear in 2 Corinthians 5.

When a person is converted they become a *new person*; the old is gone and the new has come. Our problem is that because we retain an old worldview, we allow ourselves to weaken the idea of conversion. We use the word "conversion" to describe our relationship with God in the way we would use it to describe what we have done with our attic or our loft. We have swept out the old stuff, renewed the floorboards, and turned an old and useless room into a new and usable space. That is NOT what Christian conversion means, and it is not what God is doing with the world. We need to understand the change that happens in our own life as a *new creation* and not just a reformation of our old ways. This is important because it reminds us that where once we were dead in our sins and trapped in our old ways of thinking, we are now free. There is a *new* power and presence in our lives that is stronger than the old one. We are made *new*.

Imagine that before your conversion you were watching the world in monochrome or in black and white and that at your conversion you were given the ability to see the world in high-definition colour. The new way of seeing the world not only helps you to see *better; it also helps you to see things more clearly and more vividly.* The world comes alive before your eyes. You can now *really* see the world. You can see it in a way that you could never see it before. You are different, the world is different, and everything is different.

The problem is that after our conversion we still often choose to look at the world in monochrome or in black and white instead of looking at it through the new high definition of God's grace. Although we have a new nature and a new way of looking at the world, we choose the habits of the way we used to look at the world instead of the freedom of the new way. As a *new creation* we have a new heart, a new purpose, a new life, a new meaning. We have been given a new power, a new perspective, and a new sense of meaning and significance. We have a new identity and a new intimacy with God. This is a fundamental shift in our nature, our understanding of ourselves, and our understanding of the world around us.

This *new creation* is not something that just affects us; it also affects the whole world. God's ultimate plans and purposes involve the recreation of the whole world. We hear that in the words of the Bible, such as in 1 Corinthians 15 and Romans 8 and Revelation 22. God is making all things new. There is a great difference between this and the first way in which God created. In the original creation, however God did it, he made *something* out of *nothing*. The phrase that is often used to describe this is that God created *ex nihilo*. In the new creation, God takes the substance of who we are and the substance of the world and he makes us new people and he makes a new world. That is why our lives, our bodies, and the created environment around us matter. God recreates us *as us* when he redeems us. He does not disregard who we were to make us what we are *in him*.

The same is true of the creation itself. He is intent on a *new creation*, but that new creation will spring from the old one. This means we have the joy of being involved in God's process of new creation. That joy comes from *both* experiencing the new creation in ourselves *and* being able to be conduits or channels for that new creation in the world.

We should not lose sight of this important principle. If we do, we will think that the onus of change lies *within* us in our discipleship and transformation and we will think that we are able to change the world in our own strength. This is not only untrue; it is dangerously self-reliant and has a strong scent of arrogance. We cannot change the world on our own! We cannot change ourselves on our own. We are World changers, but only in so far as we allow ourselves to be changed to be made new creations and we then allow the new power of God to flow through us to others. This is the difference between understanding that we can improve ourselves and realizing that only God can change us. It is the difference between thinking that we are the source of change and understanding that we are a conduit for the Source of change. We will return to that idea a little later in *God Gazer*.

Change from the inside out

Secondly, we must understand that true and lasting change in a human being's life never starts on the outside and works its way in. Lasting and permanent change always starts on the inside and works its way out. A person is what they think they are in their heart (Proverbs 23:7[14]). Jesus made it clear that it is not what a person does that defiles them; rather, it is what they think in their hearts, their wills, and their intentions that shape their actions and their behaviour (Matthew 15:18). By giving us the residing power and presence of the Holy Spirit after our conversion, God gives us a new heart:

> A new heart I will give you, and a new spirit I will put within you; and I will remove from your body the heart of stone and give you a heart of flesh. I will put my spirit within you and make you follow my statutes and be careful to observe my ordinances.

> **Ezekiel 36:26–27; see also Ezekiel 11:19**

---

14 The King James translation of this verse is, "For as he thinketh in his heart, so is he: Eat and drink, saith he to thee; but his heart is not with thee."

Jesus told his disciples that he would give them the Holy Spirit to live within them and to be their guide and their strength (John 14–16), and this happened on the day of Pentecost (Acts 2). In fact, there are numerous occasions in the book of Acts where the Holy Spirit was poured *into* the lives of the disciples, and this happened for many of them more than once. The change that is wrought in the lives of Christians is one that happens on the inside and works its way out – that is what King David cried out to God:

> Create in me a clean heart, O God,
> and put a new and right spirit within me.
>
> **Psalm 51:10**

God promises to give his people a new heart to know him (Jeremiah 24:7). The apostle Paul is very clear that at our conversion we are changed inwardly because something fundamentally alters in our understanding of ourselves, of God, and of the world (Romans 2:29; 12:2).

The importance of this aspect of how we understand change cannot be overstated. If we can be changed from the outside, then we can change other people and we can change ourselves, but if we cannot, then the power for true and lasting change is always something that is *given to* us and not something that we can conjure up in our own lives.

What are the implications of this? They are easy to explain. A community cannot be changed permanently by building a new school, a new hospital, and a new health centre. The change will not last because it is something that has been done *to* the people and not *in* them. The only way to see a community changed permanently is to enable the community to think differently about themselves. The power of internal change is far greater that the power of external change.

As Christians, we believe that the only way in which we can be changed internally and permanently is when God brings about that change in our lives and hearts through the Word of his Son and the power of his Spirit. This is the fundamental difference between a social gospel and the gospel as described in the Bible. No matter how hard we work, we cannot change a single person. The only One who has the power to bring about true and lasting change is Jesus Christ. He is the only One who knows us inside out and can therefore change us from the inside out. Jesus knows our thoughts and plans intrinsically because he is the Second Person of the Trinity (Matthew 9:4). God knows our thoughts and our plans (1 Chronicles 28:9; Jeremiah 17:10; Acts 1:24), and he is able to make a lasting and permanent change in our hearts which can then see that change work its way out into the world.

The power of the gospel and the power of mission

This then brings us to the nub of the issue. The gospel declares that Jesus Christ died for sin and has reconciled us to God by bearing our punishment. His death has secured our salvation. As a result of this, we are given the task of sharing this gospel by proclaiming this message. This message will change the world. As people discover this wonderful truth and believe it, they too will be changed.

This is why the local church is so central to the plans

and the purposes of God. We proclaim the life and the death of Jesus. We point to him as the only one who can bring about this permanent and lasting change. We do this hopefully and confidently, not fearfully and anxiously.

The gospel works. It changes lives, and changed lives are then used by God to change lives. We are not simply called to make a difference; we are called to make disciples. Disciples make a difference. As followers of Christ who are changed by his grace and transformed by his death and resurrection, we become people who do not simply make disciples; we also make a difference.

We make disciples by proclaiming the gospel of Jesus and teaching people to follow in his ways. We make a difference by engaging in God's mission in the world. The two are not the same thing. The gospel leads to mission. Mission flows from the gospel. We make a difference because we have experienced the power of the gospel. The change on the inside works its way out through our lives and our attitudes and our actions.

The mission of God involves us being prophetic. We speak out the word of God with boldness and with confidence. We proclaim his will and his intention. We speak out his justice (Isaiah 58; Amos 5, Micah 6:8). To be a prophetic people is to stand up for those whose voices are not heard and whose interests are ignored (Proverbs 31:8).

There is also an element of foretelling in being prophetic. We point to the promised return of Christ, we speak out God's intentions and what he is going to do in the world, and we lift up the person and the work of Jesus (John 12:32). We call all people everywhere to repent and to turn from their sin (Acts 17:30) because we know that the gospel is the power of God and it results in salvation in those who believe (Romans 1:16–17).

The mission of God also involves us being the hands and feet of Jesus. We engage in serving the poor, feeding the hungry, clothing the naked. We spend ourselves on behalf of the hungry:

> Shout out, do not hold back!
> Lift up your voice like a trumpet!
> Announce to my people their rebellion,
> to the house of Jacob their sins.
> Yet day after day they seek me
> and delight to know my ways,
> as if they were a nation that practised
> righteousness
> and did not forsake the ordinance of their God;
> they ask of me righteous judgments,
> they delight to draw near to God.
> "Why do we fast, but you do not see?
> Why humble ourselves, but you do not notice?"
> Look, you serve your own interest on your fast-day,
> and oppress all your workers.
> Look, you fast only to quarrel and to fight
> and to strike with a wicked fist.
> Such fasting as you do today
> will not make your voice heard on high.
> Is such the fast that I choose,
> a day to humble oneself?
> Is it to bow down the head like a bulrush,
> and to lie in sackcloth and ashes?
> Will you call this a fast,
> a day acceptable to the LORD?

Is not this the fast that I choose:
to loose the bonds of injustice,
to undo the thongs of the yoke,
to let the oppressed go free,
and to break every yoke?
Is it not to share your bread with the hungry,
and bring the homeless poor into your house;
when you see the naked, to cover them,
and not to hide yourself from your own kin?
Then your light shall break forth like the dawn,
and your healing shall spring up quickly;
your vindicator shall go before you,
the glory of the LORD shall be your rear guard.
Then you shall call, and the LORD will answer;
you shall cry for help, and he will say, Here I am.
If you remove the yoke from among you,
the pointing of the finger, the speaking of evil,
if you offer your food to the hungry
and satisfy the needs of the afflicted,
then your light shall rise in the darkness
and your gloom be like the noonday.
The LORD will guide you continually,
and satisfy your needs in parched places,
and make your bones strong;
and you shall be like a watered garden,
like a spring of water,
whose waters never fail.
Your ancient ruins shall be rebuilt;
you shall raise up the foundations of many
generations;
you shall be called the repairer of the breach,
the restorer of streets to live in.

If you refrain from trampling the sabbath,
from pursuing your own interests on my holy day;
if you call the sabbath a delight
and the holy day of the LORD honourable;
if you honour it, not going your own ways,
serving your own interests, or pursuing your
own affairs;
then you shall take delight in the LORD,
and I will make you ride upon the heights of
the earth;
I will feed you with the heritage of your ancestor
Jacob,
for the mouth of the LORD has spoken.

Isaiah 58

Christian faith makes a difference in the world! Where there is need and pain and loss, we are called to be there. We must not lock ourselves away from the needs we see all around us. Of course, we must avoid the mistake of getting confused between the gospel and mission. We must be gospel people and we must not make the gospel a message simply of social change. Social and political change flow from the gospel as consequences of the mission of God, but we must not think that we change the world by simply making people's lives better. We are called to a much more challenging task. We are called to see people changed from the inside out, because the impact of the gospel is transformation at every level of our lives.

Avoiding the trap of cynicism

A cynical Christian is one of the most tragic things imaginable. We who believe in Jesus and in what he has done should be known for our hope. I do not mean that we are known just as optimists, because optimists sometimes refuse to see the reality of life and run away from its harshness. I certainly do not mean that we are to be known as pessimists who refuse to see the good in the world or in the people around us and always take the negative view. No, I mean that we are *hopeful* people. We refuse cynicism as a cancer to the soul.

A Christian is someone who will keep the end in sight. A Christian remembers that history is not simply cyclical but that it is linear. The story of the planet, the story of life itself, has a beginning, a middle, and an end. We are not trapped in a ferocious cycle of repeating ourselves for eternity. Christians believe that God has broken in, and because God has broken in, we have hope. We know the end of the story, and it is simply this: *God wins.*

World changers have experienced life. World changers have come to realize that there has been a fundamental change at the very centre of their lives, and they want to share it. World changers get angry at a world that exploits people. World changers hate to see human beings treated like property. They can't help it. It is part of their new DNA. They have a message in their hearts that they need to share, and they have a passion in their lives that they can't get rid of. It gets them out of bed in the morning and it propels them through the day. They look for ways of expressing their faith and of leaving a mark. World changers are quiet revolutionaries. They want to topple systems that keep the poor entrapped. They want government to be just. They want education and care to be available to all. They want to build a better world. They want to do all of that, but they want to do more.

World changers have come to the profound realization that the only way in which a person can be permanently and fully changed is by a personal and direct encounter with the Lord Jesus Christ. Their longing is that others might experience the Life-giving power of God. They look at the world with new eyes. They don't moan about the way things are; they dream of how things could be. World changers want their lives to make a difference. They want to leave their mark. So they give God the raw materials of their own lives and they ask him to do something with them. World changers let Jesus shape their dreams. They lay their longings and their yearnings before Almighty God in an act of submission and worship. Like Moses (Exodus 4:2) and the boy with just a few loaves and fish (John 6:9), they bring what they have to Jesus. World changers lay their lives and their hopes and their dreams and their fears at the feet of Jesus and they ask him to do something with them. They bring their crooked lines to God and ask him to write straight with them. World changers bring the alabaster box of their dreams and their longings (Luke 7:36–50; Matthew 26:6–13) and they lay them at the feet of their Saviour. They give Jesus the very deepest part of themselves because it is the very deepest part of themselves that has been changed by Jesus.

Are you a World changer? Is there a dream you have of changing the world? Do you long for your life to make a difference? Do you want to see permanent and complete change in your family, your community, and your nation?

Then bring your dreams to Jesus. Lay them at the feet of the Saviour. You will never change the world, but if you let him, Jesus might just change the world through you.

> I want to be a World changer!
> A doer, not just a talker.
> I want to spread the clothes of heaven,
> no more or less than a poor man's dreams,
> beneath the feet of Jesus.

CHAPTER THIRTEEN

A Morning Many Winters Ago

I want to be a World changer
'cos on a morning many winters ago
the tomb was open
and the curse was broken.
Death had to let go
and Recreation burst out
of an old wineskin
like water from a geyser,
like the cry of a Child
pushed into the world,
and nothing
would shut him up.

Resurrection changes everything!

If the cross was how God dealt with sin and separation, then the resurrection is the way in which he demonstrates the hope and the promise of new life. The empty tomb is a trumpet call of hope, a fanfare of faith, a bold announcement of a new beginning that cannot be stopped. The raising of Jesus Christ from the dead three days after he was buried is the singular most joyous, victorious, and releasing moment the world has ever seen or will ever see.

As Christians, we are so bad at celebrating this glorious event. It shimmers and shines at the centre of our faith like a diamond, and we should declare it with boldness and confidence and faith to a world trapped in its own dimension. For years I have been saying that we should have parties every night in the week after Easter. We should light all our lights and turn up our music. We should dance in the streets. We should throw parties and write plays and films about the hope of resurrection. We should paint its message on the outside walls of our churches and we should be ablaze with colour and hopefulness. Like a child who has been born, resurrection cannot be forced backwards. It cannot be dismissed. Its cry echoes down through every generation, both backwards and forward. Backwards to the beginning of time and forward to the last moment of time as we understand it. It reverberates across every part of the universe, from the farthest reaches of the ends of the ever-expanding vastness of space to the very centre of all things.

Resurrection changes everything.

Resurrection changes you and me.

It is new life, new beginnings, new hope, new purpose, new confidence, new direction, and new heart. It is joy. The cross secures our forgiveness and the resurrection secures our freedom. It is not just a theological construct to be pondered; it is an experience to be entered, it is an encounter to be had, it is a promise to be grasped, and it is a hope to be planted. New creation starts here. New creation does not start with us; it starts with God. Our story is Christ's story. Jesus stands at the centre of humanity and he stands at the centre of history, alive and well, and it is from him that all life flows. It is because of him that all change happens.

He makes change possible, but he calls us to make change visible.

Rooted in history

In all of my enthusiasm I don't want you to miss the fact that resurrection is not just an idea for the Christian; it is a fact. We proclaim it as fact because we believe it as fact. The resurrection of Jesus Christ is rooted in history. The apostle Paul was very clear about the central importance of the historicity of Jesus being raised from the dead:

> If Christ has not been raised, your faith is futile
> and your are still in your sins. Then those also who
> have died in Christ have perished. If for this life
> only we have hoped in Christ, we are of all people
> most to be pitied.

1 Corinthians 15:17–19

The Gospel stories of Jesus' resurrection have been explored, examined, and deliberated by lawyers, journalists, and judges. Many approached them with scepticism and with a desire to disprove them, but were converted instead. People like Frank Morison, Lee Strobel and Josh McDowell were transformed by the stories of the resurrection of Jesus and have gone on to give their lives to sharing that story. I would go as far as to say that if the resurrection were proven to be a lie, then I would become a great opponent of Christianity. I would consider myself to have been duped and I would give my life to stopping others from believing in Jesus.

We must hold on to the power of the historicity of the resurrection because we must hold on to the power of the historicity of Jesus himself. I am not saying this because I am trying to reignite some kind of quest for the historical Jesus; I am saying it because Christianity is unique in its claim about God. We believe that God broke into history in human form and that he lived and walked and died among us. We also believe that he rose again. The Saviour of the world walked the land of Israel; he traversed the streets of Jerusalem. We can point to a specific time, place, and context in which our salvation was secured. This is not simply a belief or a hope; this is a historical reality, an event that took place in and around Jerusalem in the later twenties or early thirties of the first century. Do not let yourself turn it into an opinion, a theory, or an idea!

Our generation struggles with the idea of resurrection, not because we are advanced and clever and sophisticated but because every generation struggles with the idea of resurrection! Socrates (469 BC–399 BC), Plato (427 BC–327 BC), and Aristotle (384 BC–322 BC) knew that dead people did not emerge from the grave, too! It is not a normal and natural conclusion to reach. But that does not make it untrue. Every generation has dismissed the notion that Jesus could have risen from the dead: why wouldn't they? It doesn't make sense unless, of course, it is true. If it is true, then everything is changed, and we Christians believe that it is true. The early church believed that it was true. Most of them died because they believed it to be true, and you do not die for something unless you really believe it to be true.

The resurrection is the spanner in the works of logic. It is the key to understanding the victory of God in the death of Christ and it is the gateway to understanding the new creation that God has ushered in through his Son. We must not consign it to a conviction of faith spoken in the recitation of a creed but not exercising transformative power in our lives. We must preach it and proclaim it as it is – a fact of history that has never been disproven. It is the moment at which the world is changed, and we must hold on to its veracity and its historicity with all that we have, and we must challenge those in the church who dismiss it as myth and legend. To do so is to undermine the very foundation of not only our faith in Christ but also our hope for the future.

The picture of resurrection as new creation

Creation began in a garden (Genesis 1) and will end when the world becomes a Garden City (Revelation 21–22). It is fitting and apt that the new creation begins in a garden, too (John 20). In John's Gospel he tells the story of creation at the very beginning of his book and places Jesus at the very centre of it (John 1). He then relates the story of Jesus' life and ministry. When he comes to his account of the resurrection, he is very particular about how he tells it:

> Early on the first day of the week, while it was still dark, Mary Magdalene came to the tomb and saw that the stone had been removed from the tomb.

John 20:1

Those reading or hearing these words in a first-century context would immediately have recognized what John was doing. By using the phrase "early on the first day of the week", he was setting the context of Jesus' resurrection in a new creation paradigm. The tenacity and boldness of this are very powerful. The symbolism is very powerful. Here is new creation beginning in a garden. Now look forward in the story and read how Jesus revealed himself to Mary:

> She turned round and saw Jesus standing there, but
> she did not know that it was Jesus ... Supposing
> him to be the gardener...

John 20:14–15

The resurrected Jesus appears to Mary in a garden, on the first day of the week, as a Gardener! You could not have a clearer and more beautiful picture of the resurrection as the source of new creation.

This concept of resurrection as the beginning of the new creation is deeply important for us because it is the moment when Jesus bursts out of death, having defeated it (1 Corinthians 15; Ephesians 4), and he ushers in the new life of the kingdom of God. That kingdom has been pushing out from the empty tomb ever since and will continue to advance until Christ himself returns to finally and fully establish his kingdom.

The new creation will not start when Jesus returns. The new creation began when Jesus returned from the dead. That is why we read in Colossians 1:18 that the resurrection means that Jesus is the *firstborn from among the dead*. Jesus has begun a work of new creation in the resurrection, and in so doing has secured the future of the whole world. The kingdom of God in which we now live and which we make manifest to those around us was ushered in by the life, death, and resurrection of Jesus, and absolutely nothing can stop it.

There is another aspect of John's resurrection narrative that I want to highlight. It comes from the beginning and the end of his Gospel and is directly connected to John 1 and John 20. I have written of it many times, but it is worth repeating here because it is so important.

At the beginning of the Gospel of John we read:

> The light shines in the darkness, and the darkness did not overcome it.
>
> **John 1:5**

The word translated "did not overcome" is actually a very difficult word to translate in English. It is written in a tense that means "did, does and will". In other words, we could translate the verse like this:

> The light shines in the darkness, and the darkness never did, never does, and never will overcome it.
>
> **(My translation)**

If we look at the meaning of the word itself rather than just its tense, we discover that it means a whole range of things, including overcome, comprehend, change, conceal, diminish, destroy, explain, and reduce. So let's try and translate it again:

> The light shines in the darkness, and the darkness never did, never does and never will overcome it,

> change it, alter it, conceal it, diminish it, destroy
> it, remove it, explain it, obstruct it, overpower it,
> comprehend it, encompass it, be stronger than it…

> **(My translation)**

I have spent twenty-five years trying to understand this one phrase in the Bible, and I have to tell you that I am unable to. Every single time I read it, I weep, and it causes me to worship. It sends a shiver down my spine and it stretches my mind. It grips my imagination. I have had this phrase given to me in art form and it hangs in my office. I think about it every single day because it is so powerful. The light cannot be overcome by the darkness! Hallelujah!

Why, then, does John choose to say in John 20:

> Early on the first day of the week, while it was still
> dark…

> **John 20:1**

If the light cannot be overcome by the darkness, what is happening here? It's obvious, isn't it? They think Jesus is still dead. The light has gone out. Jesus is not dead, however, and the light has not gone out! The light has overcome the darkness. The light has defeated the darkness. The light has overpowered the darkness because the light is stronger than the darkness! Resurrection has begun. Light is pushing out darkness. New life has burst out of the ground and nothing will be able to stop it. This is why resurrection is so important to us as Christians. It is the very ground from which our hope springs. It is the soil in which our promise of new life for ourselves has been planted.

Here are some of the profound implications of resurrection for us:

- Resurrection is a declaration of new creation.
- Resurrection is the destruction of death.
- Resurrection is the defeat of fear.
- Resurrection is a demonstration of hope.
- Resurrection is a denuding of darkness.

We simply cannot overestimate the significance of this moment for those of us who want to be World changers. We must allow it to inspire us every day. When the world seems trapped in darkness and sin and despair, we remember that Jesus is alive.

Are you trapped? Do you feel like you are in a place of darkness? Do you feel as though the light has gone out? Are you feeling the chains of death, the fear of the darkness? Then allow the power of the resurrection to inspire you again. Read the story slowly and let it fill you up with hope. Don't give in. Don't give up. Don't throw in the towel. Let the power of the resurrection inspire you and renew you again.

World changers know we don't have the power to change the world, but we know a Man who does. World changers know that the same power that raised Jesus from the dead now lives in them (Ephesians 1, 3). World changers have tasted the resurrection power of Christ in their own lives and they have seen it in the lives of others. World changers have identified with the resurrection in their baptism and now want to live in the resurrection power of Jesus before the world. World changers know that the only power that can change the world is the power of the One who defeated death and rose again. World changers want to apply the power of resurrection in every area of their lives and of their communities. World changers don't want to keep this message for themselves; they want to share it.

The Church of Jesus Christ is a community of World changers. Or at least, it is supposed to be.

The vanguard's on the move

> I want to be a World changer
> because it's started…
> because the vanguard's on the move…
> and Love is pushing out hate
> and Light is shining out
> and darkness can't understand It,
> beat It,
> change It,
> hide It,
> kill It,
> stop It,
> win.

The church of Jesus Christ is alive and well across the world today and being used by God to bring about the most remarkable transformation on the planet. Millions upon millions of people receive help, support, love, care, and protection through the church. While much of the press around us dismisses the church or mocks us, God is using the church to change the world. Don't believe the bad press. We are broken and flawed and we make mistakes and we pick the wrong fights and we say the wrong things, but the church is the vanguard of God's kingdom. We must never forget it. We are World changers.

Our future is more certain than our past. We are not simply moving forward; we are being drawn forward by the power of God. The resurrection took place 2,000 years ago and it propels us into the future God has for us, but God has also gone ahead into our future and he is drawing us forward in his purposes and his plans. If the first coming of Jesus Christ was the great event at the centre of history and the creation is the great event at the beginning of it, then the physical, visible, and bodily return of the resurrected Christ is the great event at the end of history. It will usher in the final and the complete consummation of God's purposes and kingdom.

We, the church, are the advance party for this kingdom. In our daily lives we demonstrate its existence and its power. God is at work through his church!

That means your life matters and your choices matter and you matter. It is so easy to be lost in the detail of our daily lives and to miss the bigger picture of God's plans and purposes in the world, but we must try to lift our heads. Take a look at Jesus once again and remind yourself of the wonderful privilege that you have to be in his family and part of his army. Your ordinary everyday life can make a tremendous difference. The world is not changed by superstars; it is changed by ordinary people like you and me living in a way that brings pleasure to God and displays him to the world around us. Your life is a great adventure of faith in which you follow the direction of God and allow yourself to be caught in the wind and the purpose of the Holy Spirit.

The adventure of faith

There is no safer place to be than in the centre of God's will for your life. There is nothing that will bring you greater happiness than to be in communion with God and doing what he has called you to do. Being the person that he has destined you to be is the most rewarding, life-giving experience imaginable. Continue on the journey. Don't give up!

God's purpose in the world is its utter transformation, and you have a part to play. As a saint of God you are called to display his praises (1 Peter 2:9). Whether you work in an office, a school, a shop, or a church, your life can be an adventure. God can change the world through you! It is as we live for him that we can make the greatest difference, and it is as we live for him that we are truly alive. God does not promise you an easy life. He does not promise that people will applaud you. You may even have to suffer and die for the faith you hold, but I promise you that you can leave a mark.

As you surrender your plans and your purposes and your future to God, he will take you on the most remarkable journey. I surrendered my life to him almost thirty years ago. Since then I have preached in more than fifty countries to more than two million people. I am amazed at the journey God has taken me on. I have stood before Prime Ministers and presidents. From the Houses of Parliament in London to the United Nations in New York, I cannot believe what God has led me into. I have stood with the poor in Bangladesh and preached to the rich in Hampshire. I have held children as they died and had the privilege of dedicating new lives to God. I have baptized thousands, married hundreds, buried many, and preached all over the world. I would never have dreamed this was possible. I have the privilege of pastoring a group of people I love. I lead a Christian event that is becoming a movement. I get to write books! My life is completely different to what I would have thought it would look like. Why? For one reason only: Jesus Christ has taken hold of my heart and taken hold of my imagination and taken hold of me.

You might be the one whom God chooses to use to change someone else's life and destiny. Your words and actions can change the world if you let them become God's actions and words. Let him take hold of you. Let him draw you into the most remarkable adventure of faith. Let him in. Take time to look at him – to really look – and as you do, allow what you see to change your life.

It is worth it. I promise.

> I want to be a World changer
> because there's safety in this danger.
> There's meaning in this purpose.
> There's joy in this mission
> and too many others are missing
> the power of life in all its fullness.

God Gazer, Life Giver, World Changer

World changer? Life giver? God gazer?
God, break in – then break out.
Fill me – then make me leak.
Plug me in and push me out.
In me, through me, around me.
Make me a Patrick!
Make me a Brendan!
God gazing, Life giving, World changing!
Captured by the brilliance
that springs from the radiance
of you!

Thank you.
Thank you for taking the time to read my book.
Thank you for pausing along the way to think and to pray.

Thank you for opening your heart.

Thank you for allowing the Holy Spirit to speak to you.

Thank you for what you do for the kingdom of God.

Thank you for being faithful in the small things.

Thank you for your giving.

Thank you for your sacrifice.

Thank you for your commitments.

I am inspired by people who give their ordinary lives to God and allow him to use them. I meet them all the time in small churches and hidden places. They are not well known, but they are heroes of faith nevertheless. Perhaps I have met you somewhere and your story inspired some of this book. Perhaps we have not met yet. Who knows?

I know this, though: it is as we give ourselves to God's purposes and plans that we are most content. The world around us desperately needs to see ordinary Christians like you live in extraordinary ways. The early Celtic saints inspire me – people like Patrick who gave his whole life to seeing the gospel change Ireland, and people like Brendan who set out on an adventure that most of us would consider madness. Yet it is the Brendans and Patricks of this world that change it. They push into new territory and they do new things. They do small things with great faithfulness, and they do great things with great care.

I've written this simple blessing for you:

> *May God give you a fresh vision of his beauty and majesty.*
> *May he overwhelm you with his love.*
> *In the moments when you need him most, may you sense him most deeply.*
> *May you see new things in him every day.*
> *May your love for him deepen.*
> *May your yearning and hunger for him intensify.*
> *May you be changed by an encounter with the loving, holy God.*

May your deepest yearning be for him.
May you know his love so deeply that it scatters your deepest fears and dispels your darkest darkness.
May your life revolve around the brilliance of the Son of God.
May God shine out through you.
May he continually fill you and renew you.
May others see him in you.
May they hear him through you.
May they feel his touch through your hand and your embrace.
May your life make a difference in the world.
May the God of grace give you grace to live.
May the God of hope give you hope to believe.
May the God of power give you power to stand.
May the God of new beginnings give you a new beginning.
May the God who made you, keep you.
May the God who leads you, guide you.
May the God of purpose give you fresh and new purpose.
May the God of new beginnings begin a new work in you.
May the God of perfect complete his work in you.
May the God who is there, fill you.
May the God who was present when you took your first breath, welcome you into his presence when you take your last breath.
May you be a God gazer.
May you be a Life giver.
May you be a World changer.
Amen.

Keep in Touch

I would love to keep in touch with you and hear of ways in which *God Gazer* has helped, encouraged, or inspired you, or ways in which you have used it on your own or with others. I look forward to connecting with you. If you are ever in a place where I am preaching, come and say hello, or just get in touch.

Email: Malcolm.duncan@goldhill.org
Twitter: @MalcolmJDuncan
Facebook: MalcolmJDuncan
Web: www.goldhill.org
Blog: www.malcolmduncan.typepad.com

#Godgazer